GLOSSARY OF BRITISH-AMERICAN EQUIVALENTS

Button-through skirt = Buttoned skirt
Bodkin = Needle
Collar and revers = Notched collar
Elasticated = Elasticized
Grandfather collar = Stand-up collar
Machine (verb) = Machine stitch
Oversew = Slipstitch
Petersham = Thick corded ribbon used to stiffen belts
Quick-unpick = Seam ripper
Revers = Lapels
Spool = Bobbin
Tack = Baste
Tacking Stitches = Basting stitches
Zip = Zipper

Sterling Publishing Co., Inc. New York

Published in 1987 by
Sterling Publishing Co., Inc.
Two Park Avenue
New York, N.Y. 10016

ISBN 0-8069-6656-4 (hardcover)
ISBN 0-8069-6634-3 (paper)

First published in Great Britain in 1986.
Published by arrangement with Martin Books, an imprint of Woodhead-Faulkner Ltd, Cambridge, in association with Style Patterns Ltd.
Printed and bound in Italy.

Contents

Dear Home Dressmaker,

Hello! Welcome to this course of dressmaking lessons. You may have no dressmaking experience at all, or you may be familiar with basic dressmaking techniques. It doesn't matter. Follow this sewing course through from the beginning and, whatever your standard of sewing, you will learn something new. And, more important, I hope that from these dressmaking lessons you will learn to *enjoy* making your own clothes.

Dressmaking can be a very absorbing hobby. At its best, it is using fabric creatively in the way that an artist uses brushes and paint, combining the elements of colour, fabric, proportion and line in clothes that are delightful to wear and pleasing to look at. At its worst, it is an unsatisfactory combination of poor fabric, bad line and incorrect proportion in clothes that cover the body to keep it warm, but do nothing to delight the eye or flatter the figure.

The majority of home dressmakers who are self-taught have often had to struggle through this second stage to achieve the first. They have learned by trial and error, and usually by leaving a trail of rejected garments on the way! The aim of this book is therefore to help you achieve the results you want with your home dressmaking, cutting out some of the failure and frustration on the way. You will still have some disappointments – clothes that don't look as you imagined they would and that you do not enjoy wearing – but isn't it the same, anyway, with the clothes that you buy?

Eventually, with practice and experience in making your own clothes, you will become knowledgeable about fabrics, develop an awareness of those styles which flatter you and become selective about fashion and design. You will also become very critical of the finish of any clothes that you buy. You will get to the stage where you would much rather make your own clothes than buy them. This is a happy stage: you can have the style you like, the fabric you enjoy wearing, in the colour you want, made up in the design which flatters you. And all for much less than you would have to pay to buy second-best from the shop rail (shop rack).

Another big plus about home dressmaking is that you can get engrossed in a creative hobby which is productive as well as satisfying. Like any other creative pastime, dressmaking is therapeutic – or it should be. If you find you are getting irritated or frustrated with your sewing, then stop and leave it for a while. Take a break from it and make a cup of coffee, or take a walk round the garden. You should be able to lose yourself in your sewing to the exclusion of everything else, so that it can be an escape as well as a relaxation. Try not to sew when you are tired. And make time to sew by giving it an important place in your routine – let it take precedence over the housework! The more you sew, the better you will get and the more you will enjoy it.

And since the more you sew, the more you will learn, ask yourself whether you need to neaten *all* those inside seams so meticulously. Wouldn't you be better employed starting to cut out and sew something new?

So go ahead and make a start on these sewing lessons. If you can, devote a definite time each week to learning to sew. In the first few lessons we will discuss patterns, fabrics and what you will need to help you with your dressmaking, including sewing machines. Then we will make a start on a very simple pattern – one you can master easily – and progress to something more adventurous. Each of the dressmaking procedures is explained very clearly as it is introduced, so I hope that you will get a feeling of achievement and satisfaction as you learn.

This is *your* dressmaking course: *enjoy it*!

Leila Aitken.

LESSON ONE

Choosing your pattern

Now that you have made the decision to start to sew, I hope that you are going to enjoy *all* the dressmaking procedures that you will come across in this book. But to my mind, the initial stage of opening a pattern catalogue to choose your pattern from the enticing display of colourful fashion sketches and photographs is one of the most exciting.

What will you make? There to choose from are extreme fashions copying the latest designer looks, more conservative designs from which you can safely choose and High Street* fashions very similar to the designs which you will see currently in shop windows.

What I suggest you do is try to get hold of an out-of-date STYLE pattern catalogue. A new pattern catalogue is issued to the pattern counters of your fabric shop several times a year. Many shops sell the out-of-date catalogues for a nominal sum and others will be happy to give you one for nothing. You can pass many happy hours browsing through your catalogue, learning your way around it, and as you do so you will be absorbing fashion looks, colour combination, proportion and even ideas for accessorising your clothes. Some of the patterns in your catalogue will obviously be out of date as nearly 50 new designs are introduced with each new issue. But it still remains valuable to you in many other respects.

STYLE also produce a smaller quarterly catalogue which you can buy from pattern departments and some newsagents, or have sent direct to your home. It is not expensive, features some of the latest designs and it also contains sewing hints and useful information, special offers and mail order patterns. So browse through the patterns and enjoy them, and make a note of those that you particularly like and aim one day to make! Despite the enticing selection of patterns available, I think that it is a good idea for a beginner to start with a *skirt*.

A skirt is a good introduction to dressmaking because it introduces you to cutting out with the minimum of complications and not too many pattern pieces. It involves several basic sewing techniques, including a zip, a waistband and a hem, which are satisfying and straightforward to learn, and it does not involve those techniques which need extra care and practice to look professional – fine edges or shaped collars, for example. So let's have a look at some of the designs from the skirt section of the STYLE pattern book.

*Main Street.

WHAT'S YOUR LINE?

Skirt shapes, as you will have seen, have changed dramatically in recent years. A skirt is no longer either straight or A-line, although these are still popular shapes. The choice is now very wide: there are skirts which swirl with fine pleats from the hipline, skirts which drape, with bias-cut panels, skirts which fall into soft folds gathered at the waistline, and pencil-slim skirts with flared panels inserted at the hemline to give a lean, elegant line; there are wrap skirts and button-through skirts, side-buttoned skirts and even skirts which button down the back.

In this very wide selection there must be several which will suit *you*. How do you know which they are?

First of all, you have to take a good hard look at yourself and identify this elusive thing called *line*. Some sewing manuals simply tell you to identify your 'figure type' and choose your pattern accordingly. Although we shall come back to that when we start to take measurements, that isn't the whole story. Line is difficult to define, but what you are aiming at in dressmaking is not only to understand your figure type to disguise its faults and emphasise its good points, but also to achieve a pleasing *all-over* silhouette, a good line, a total look. You are, in fact, creating and choosing to create a shape or a style.

You have to decide what kind of person you are – or want to be – which lines are right for you and which lines create an effect that you are unhappy with. If you see yourself as soft and feminine, you will choose fluid, unstructured lines. If you see yourself as brisk and efficient, you will choose clean, tailored lines. You have to interpret the effect you would like to create. If you see yourself as extrovert and bubbly, then you will tend to choose a flounced and gathered skirt. Should you want to feel languid and elegant, then you will go for a slim line in a longer length. If you are daring and innovative, then you will go for the latest designer looks, and if you are strictly practical, then no doubt you will choose an easy, comfortable line, such as an all-round pleated skirt.

Age, incidentally, has nothing whatsoever to do with it! Age does not restrict your choice of style, as there is no such thing as a 'young' style. What *is* ageing is still wearing the lines that you adopted 10 years ago. Age does, however, bring with it the experience and confidence to know which lines are the most flattering for *you*.

While you are leafing through the skirt section of the pattern catalogue, try to make up your *own* mind what sort of skirt you want to make. Don't ask a friend to help you. In the end, you will learn more about the lines which flatter you and the type of clothes you feel good in if you work it out for yourself. One good tip is that the patterns you are immediately drawn to and are enthusiastic about are usually the ones that you will enjoy wearing and will not tire of. Trust your initial reactions and if you feel very undecided about a design, leave it and choose something else.

Once you have decided on your skirt pattern, you have to work out the *size* of pattern you will need.

HOW DO YOU MEASURE UP?

The present fashions make this an ideal time to learn to sew. Close fitting, figure-hugging designs are not the most popular and so a great deal of tedious and complicated pattern alteration is no longer necessary. Many styles are easy, loose-fitting and unstructured and so very detailed body measurement is also unnecessary.

There are certain essential body measurements on which your pattern size is based. You must take these measurements very accurately and from them select the pattern size which corresponds most nearly to your own measurements. There is a chart at the back of the STYLE pattern catalogues detailing all the different pattern measurements and we will refer to that later. But the first thing is to take your measurements.

How to take your measurements
If you can, get a friend to help you to measure up. Stand up looking straight ahead and *relax* – don't hold your breath or hold your tummy in! Remove outer garments and take your measurements in your slip. Hold the tape snugly but not tightly, and if you are not yet completely happy with metric measurements, then take your measurements in both metric and imperial to familiarise yourself with both.

Remember that the pattern is based on the *actual* measurements which you are taking, so do be accurate. The pattern designer adds on an allowance for what is known as 'ease' and this gives you the room to move comfortably. *You* must take your measurements exactly. STYLE patterns will give you a very satisfactory fit if you take your measurements in this way.

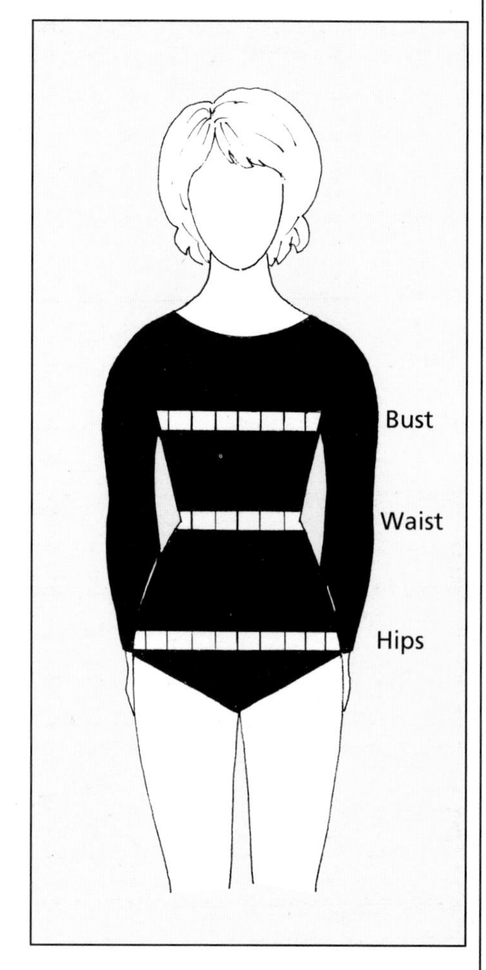

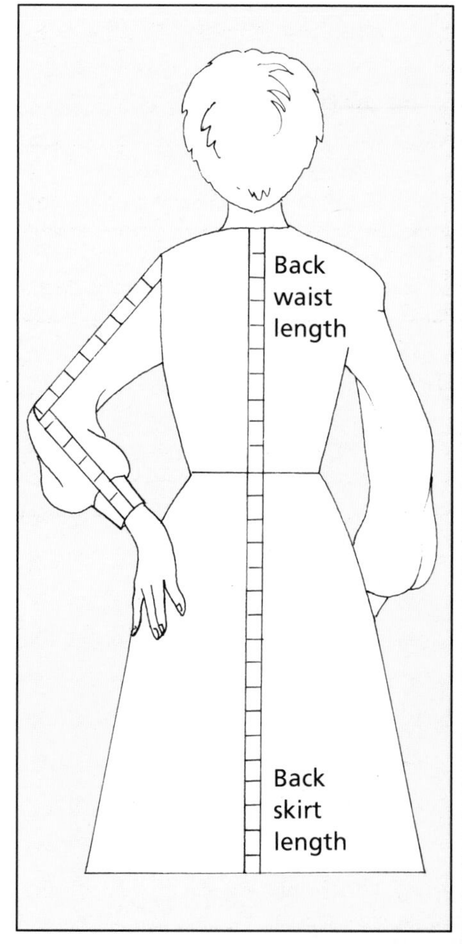

Use the Personal Measurement Chart opposite to fill in your measurements (in pencil).

YOUR PERSONAL MEASUREMENT CHART to help you select the pattern type and size for your figure

Name ______________________________

Date ______________________________

Height (without shoes) ______________________________

	Metric (centimetres)	Imperial (inches)
Body measurements **Bust** Around fullest part, straight across back, high under the arm		
Waist Comfortably, at natural waistline		
Hips Around fullest part, 18–23 cm (7–9 in) below waist		
Other measurements (to compare with the pattern measurement) **Sleeve length (*a*) Shoulder to elbow** **(*b*) Elbow to wrist** Take with arm bent to establish correct location of sleeve darts		
Back waist length From prominent bone at back neck base to waistline		
Back skirt length From waistline to bottom of skirt, down centre back		

These measurements show

my figure type is ______________________________

in pattern size ______________________________

Finding your correct pattern size
Now turn to the *back* of the STYLE pattern catalogue. There you will find a chart giving the measurements for the standard pattern sizings. They are divided into figure 'types', and the two 'types' from which you will select your own pattern size are *Misses* and *Women*.

Remember to fill in your pattern size and figure type on your personal measurement chart. Obviously, your personal measurements are not *exactly* the same as those listed below, and this is where multi-sized patterns are a boon. These have several consecutive sizes printed on the same pattern and have the advantage that you can cut out a dress using one size for the bust and a larger size on the hip, for example.

For easy-fitting and full skirts, the hip measurement is obviously not as important as the waist measurement, so select your skirt pattern size by your waist measurement. For slim-fitting and straight skirts, choose your pattern by your hip measurement. It is easy to alter the waist of a pattern, but, for a beginner, it is not so easy to alter a pattern at the hip.

When you have determined your figure type and pattern size, you can go ahead and choose your pattern with confidence.

MISSES' AND WOMEN'S SIZING CHARTS

MISSES

Misses' patterns are designed for a well proportioned and developed figure, about 165–168 cm (5'5" to 5'6") without shoes.

Size	8	10	12	14	16	18	20	22	24	
Imperial measurements										
Bust	31½	32½	34	36	38	40	42	44	46	in
Waist	24	25	26½	28	30	32	34	37	39	in
Hip	33½	34½	36	38	40	42	44	46	48	in
Back waist length	15¾	16	16¼	16½	16¾	17	17¼	17⅜	17½	in
Metric measurements										
Bust	80	83	87	92	97	102	107	112	117	cm
Waist	61	64	67	71	76	81	87	94	99	cm
Hip	85	88	92	97	102	107	112	117	122	cm
Back waist length	40	40.5	41.5	42	42.5	43	44	44	44.5	cm

WOMEN

Women's patterns are designed for the larger, more fully mature figure, about 165–168 cm (5'5" to 5'6") without shoes.

Size	40	42	44	46	48	
Imperial measurements						
Bust	44	46	48	50	52	in
Waist	37	38	41½	44	46½	in
Hip	46	48	50	52	54	in
Back waist length	17⅜	17½	17⅝	17¾	17⅞	in
Metric measurements						
Bust	112	117	122	127	132	cm
Waist	94	99	105	112	118	cm
Hip	117	122	127	132	137	cm
Back waist length	44	44.5	45	45	45.5	cm

SIMPLE PATTERN ALTERATION

The only pattern alteration you may need to use at this stage is *adding on* to a pattern at the waistline, if you are making a slim skirt and the waist measurement of the pattern is smaller than your own. (If the pattern is too large at the waist, reduce it at the *fitting stage* rather than now, since you cannot put back any fabric you have cut off!)

Increasing a pattern at the waist

The addition is made at the side seams. Pin extra tissue paper to the pattern margin at the side seams of both the back and front skirt pattern pieces.

Divide the amount you wish to add to the pattern by four, as you are working on a quarter of the pattern. For example, if you need to add a total of 5 cm (2 in), you will add 1.2 cm (½ in) to each side seam. Measure this amount outside the seamline at the waist and draw the new cutting line from this point, curving in very gradually back on to the original line at the hip (Fig 1.1).

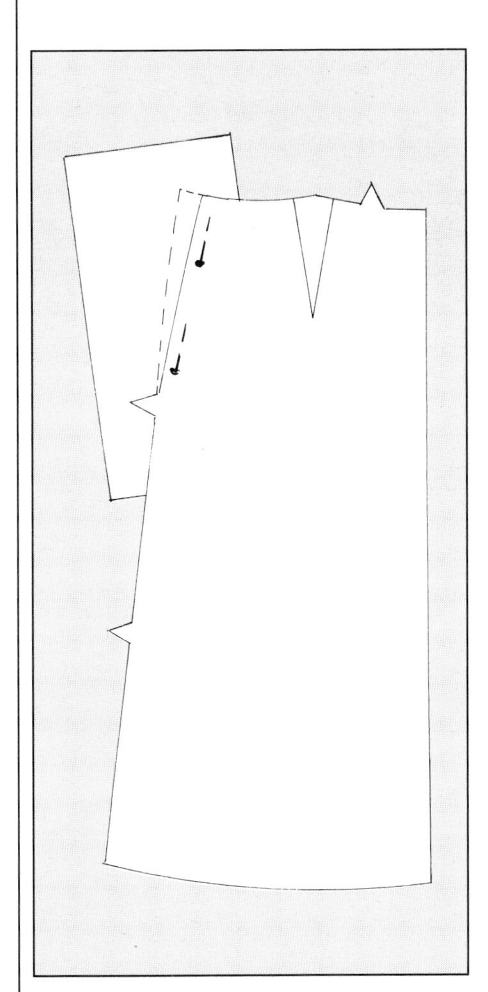

Fig 1.1 Increasing a pattern at the waist.

Remember that if you do add on to the pattern at the waist, you will also need to extend the waistband by that amount.

Adjusting the skirt length

Have a look at the back of the envelope. At the very end of the list of sizings and fabric requirements you will find the *finished length* of the skirt you are making. Compare this with the *back skirt length* you have written on your measurement chart. The paper pattern must be altered accordingly, but err on the safe side if you are going to shorten a pattern!

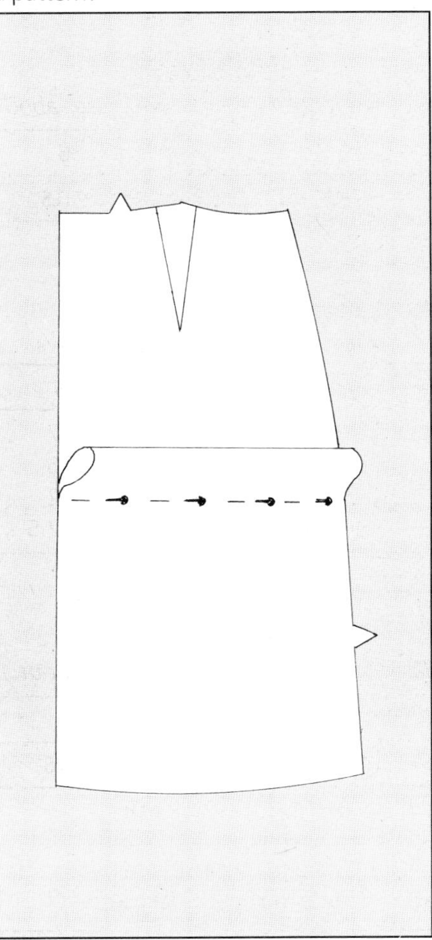

Fig 1.2 Shortening a pattern.

Shortening a pattern

There is a line clearly marked on the skirt pattern indicating where any alteration must be made. If the skirt is very flared or A-line, this line will be just below the hip. If the skirt is fairly straight, this line will be at the hem itself.

Shortening a skirt is a simple matter of folding up the tissue paper by the amount you wish to remove on the line indicated (Fig 1.2).

Lengthening a pattern

Cut the pattern out along the marked line. Place a strip of paper underneath the pieces, wider than the amount you wish to add. Move the pattern pieces apart by the required amount and Sellotape the tissue to the strip of paper (Fig 1.3).

On the back of the pattern envelope you will also find a helpful list of fabric suggestions for that particular pattern, so read this through before you go on to the next exciting stage of choosing your fabric.

Fig 1.3 Lengthening a pattern.

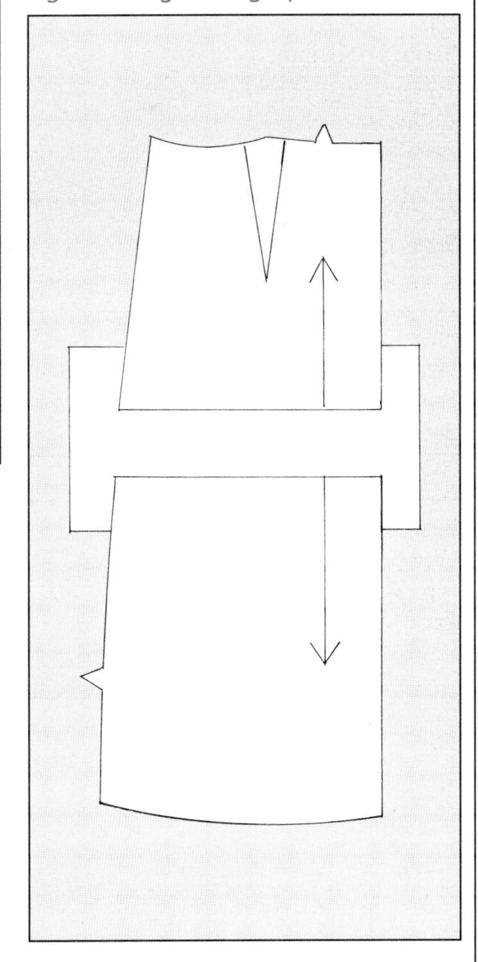

LESSON TWO

Choosing your fabric and sewing equipment

FABRICS

Choosing fabric is a very personal thing, but there are several guidelines which may help you. First, try to get really interested in fabric. Browse round a good fabric department and learn all you can about fabrics. Learn to recognise different types of fabric, handle them if you can and learn about different fabric weights, and drape any fabric when you get the chance to see how it behaves. You will learn to love different materials and become very excited about new designs, colours and texture.

There are so many excellent fabrics to choose from these days that becoming more knowledgeable about fabrics can sometimes make the task of choosing your fabric more difficult. As a start, refer to the back of your pattern envelope. The types of fabrics suitable for making up that pattern are listed, so this is a good guide.

Fabric is manufactured in two basic ways: it is either woven or knitted. You therefore have to make a choice between these types right away. The simplest woven fabric is constructed by two groups of yarns woven at right angles. The warp or lengthwise threads which are put up first are the strongest threads and run parallel to the selvage. The weft or crosswise threads run over and under the warp. There are then many variations of this weave resulting in interesting fabric textures.

Knitted fabrics are made from continuous yarn knitted into interlocking loops, which gives a fabric with some degree of stretch. The weights of knitted fabrics vary considerably, and two terms which you may encounter are 'denier', denoting the weight and the thickness of the fabric, and 'gauge', which refers to the number of stitches used.

Both these types of fabric are suitable for beginners and both are suitable for you to make up into a skirt. It is a matter of personal preference which you choose. Woven fabrics are easy to handle and they press well. Knitted fabrics drape beautifully, give a fluid line and generally do not crease.

Another choice you have to make is between natural fabrics (wool, cotton, silk and linen) and synthetic fibres (polyester, acrylic, rayon and many other trade names). Man-made fabrics are now so good that the choice between the two is difficult. Natural fibres breathe, press well and are absorbent. Man-made fibres do not crush readily, and they wear well and keep their shape. A mixture of the two – for example, polyester/cotton and polyester/ wool – is often a splendid combination, as the best qualities of both are combined in the one fabric.

When trying to make up your mind about your fabric, open out the fabric from the bale and drape it against yourself. Any fabric, opened out, looks very different from when it is rolled round a board. As with your pattern, your *initial* reaction to any fabric is a good guide. Always choose a fabric that you are really enthusiastic about right from the start.

Be adventurous in your choice and look for cleverly co-ordinating fabrics. There are now many manufacturers who are making complete ranges of delightfully co-ordinated materials. So, although at the moment you are only aiming to make a skirt, keep an eye open for colour and pattern co-ordinates for the fabric you choose. This will help to achieve a professional finish and give a 'designer' look to your clothes.

On the subject of colour
Whether we recognise it or not, colour plays a very important part in our lives, and one of the bonuses of making your own clothes is that you can wear the colours that *you* enjoy looking at. You need no longer be dictated to by the 'fashion colour of the year'. You need no longer wear puce or damson when the shop windows are full of it and you have a high colour and broken veins!

Hold fabrics up against your face to see how well they suit you; some *will* do more for you than others. But, as well as choosing a colour that flatters you, do choose colours that you personally enjoy and that you find stimulating or soothing, or that cheer you up, because colour can do all these things.

Revel in the lovely selection and mixture of colours in fabrics. You don't have to play safe in navy any more or choose black because 'it never goes wrong'.

How much fabric will you need?
Go back to your pattern envelope. There are probably several versions of the skirt you wish to make on the same pattern. These are known as 'views'. Decide on the view you prefer, ascertain your chosen fabric width, turn to the back of the envelope and there you will find a table detailing the amount of fabric you need to buy. But there is one complication, and that is a thing called *nap*.

Nap fabrics
Nap fabrics are fabrics which have a pile. Velvet is a good example. When you smooth the pile of velvet in one direction, it lies flat; when you smooth it in the other direction, it stands up and looks a completely different colour. So it is obvious that when you sew with velvet, you will have to cut it out with all the pattern pieces lying in one direction.

The term 'nap' is also applied to all those fabrics which have a one-way design – for example, a floral fabric where all the flowers grow in one direction. This must also be cut out with the design running one way. You will often see references to 'nap fabric and one-way designs' and that is what they mean.

So take a good look at your fabric: if it has a pattern on it, reverse it to see if it is a one-way design; if it is a brushed fabric, even if only slightly, it will have nap. If you have chosen a nap fabric, you will need to buy extra material to allow you to place the pattern pieces on in one direction. You will find the amount you need for nap fabric is also listed on the back of your pattern envelope.

So far we have only dealt with the back of the envelope, and we will shortly open it! But before that, it is a good idea to collect together some of the equipment you will need.

SEWING MACHINES

The most important piece of equipment for any dressmaker is her sewing machine. It can make all the difference in the world to your enjoyment of dressmaking: a good sewing machine is a delight to use; an inferior sewing machine is a source of irritation and frustration.

If you have an old sewing machine and have always adopted the attitude 'Oh, it will do for me, for all the sewing I do', don't be *too* complacent about it! Go out and have a look at the wide range of up-to-date machines available and discover how many dressmaking chores they can deal with, with ease. Get yourself the best machine you can afford. It is a common mistake to think that you will not use all the facilities on an advanced machine. You may not, if you do not take the trouble to study your machine and familiarise yourself with what it can do. But I am assuming that, since you have taken the trouble to buy this book, you are enthusiastic about learning to sew and will spend time on it and on your sewing machine.

There used to be just three basic types of sewing machine. Now, there are three basic types plus computerised machines. If you can afford it, a computerised machine is certainly the answer, even for a beginner – in fact, especially for a beginner. Computerised machines are fun and they are very simple to use. They will tack and tailor tack, stitch an infinite variety of excellent seams and stitches, do top-stitching and saddle-stitching, and produce effortless buttonholes and embroidery, all at the touch of a button.

The other types of sewing machine available are as follows:

1 Basic zig-zag machines. These will do straight stitching and zig-zag for neatening seams, satin stitching and somewhat laborious buttonholes.

2 Semi-automatic machines. In addition to the features of the basic machines above, these machines have a choice of decorative stitches and stretch stitches and will do semi-automatic buttonholes.

3 Fully automatic machines. These machines are capable of a wide variety of stitches and seam finishes and an easy, automatic buttonhole. The price you pay determines how much the machine can do. At the top of the price range, fully automatic machines have electronic foot control and powerful needle penetration even at the slowest speeds which produces superb stitching.

Always study the handbook for whichever machine you use. It contains useful tips on general sewing as well as giving uses for the various stitches.

When using your machine, you will find it helpful to remember the following points:

1 The commonest cause of trouble is having the machine threaded up incorrectly. So unthread it and rethread it, checking the instructions in the machine handbook. Another common cause of trouble is having the needle inserted either the wrong way round or not high enough. Again, you will find an illustration of how the needle should be inserted into the machine in the handbook.

2 When you remove the fabric from the machine, pull it towards the back and *always* leave the thread take-up lever at its highest position, so that the next movement of the needle is downwards. This will prevent it unthreading and also prevent you from getting a tangle of threads in the shuttle raceway. The formation of a stitch is completed only when the take-up lever is at its highest point. If you start to sew with the take-up lever in its 'down' position, a tangle of three threads is often formed, and the machine will 'buzz' when you press the foot pedal to start to sew.

3 Don't fiddle with the tension! You should be able to stitch most fabrics, even very fine ones, without adjusting the tension. Modern sewing machines do not need constant fiddling with the tension screw, so adjust this only as a last resort.

4 It is important to choose the appropriate needle and the correct stitch length for your fabric: for example, heavy denim will require a stronger needle and a larger stitch than a chiffon, which requires a fine needle and a very small stitch. The higher the number of the sewing machine needle, the heavier and thicker it is. Ball-point needles are excellent for knit fabrics and man-made fibres.

5 Regularly brush out the shuttle raceway with the brush provided. Don't let fluff and threads accumulate as this will cause problems.

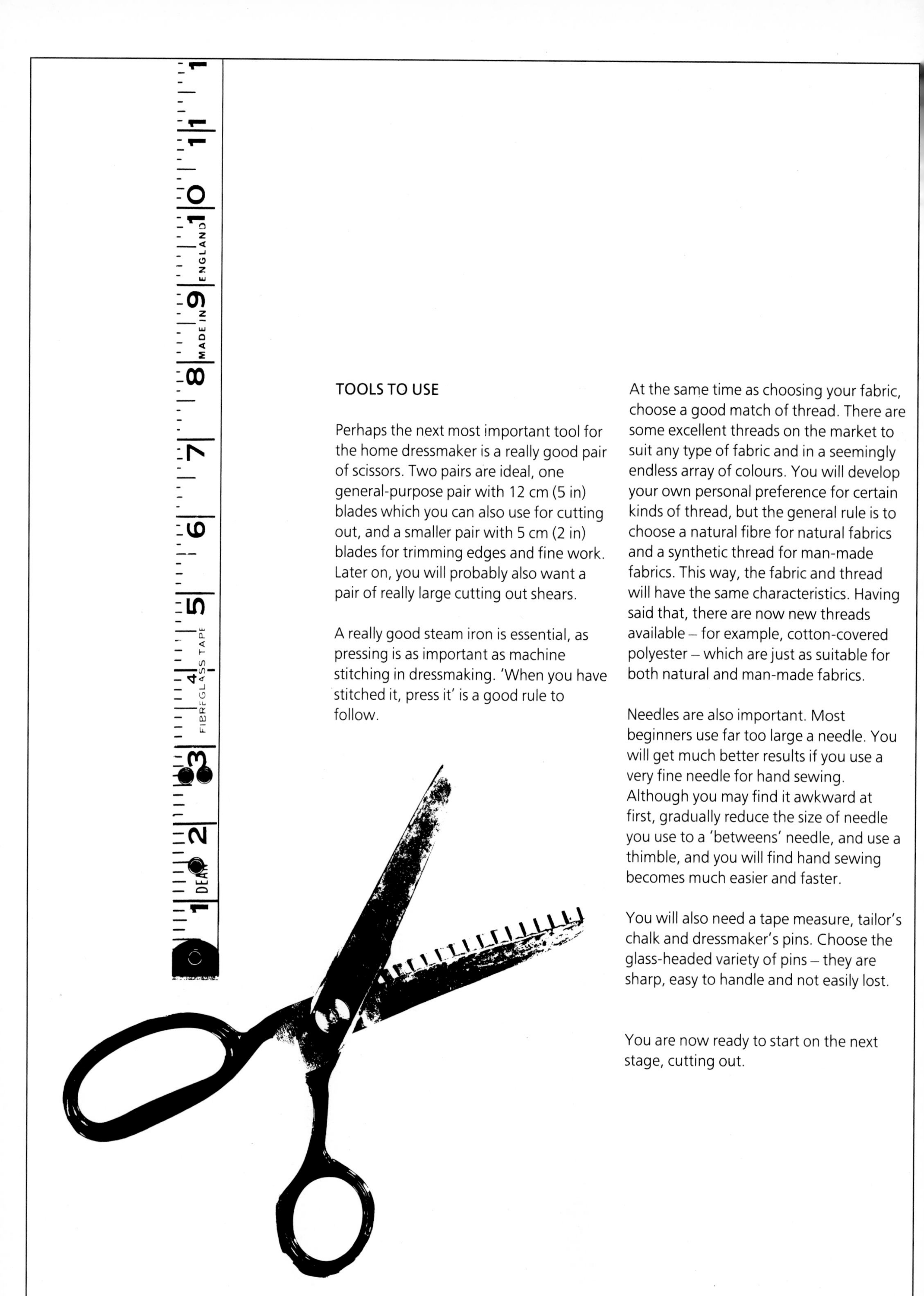

TOOLS TO USE

Perhaps the next most important tool for the home dressmaker is a really good pair of scissors. Two pairs are ideal, one general-purpose pair with 12 cm (5 in) blades which you can also use for cutting out, and a smaller pair with 5 cm (2 in) blades for trimming edges and fine work. Later on, you will probably also want a pair of really large cutting out shears.

A really good steam iron is essential, as pressing is as important as machine stitching in dressmaking. 'When you have stitched it, press it' is a good rule to follow.

At the same time as choosing your fabric, choose a good match of thread. There are some excellent threads on the market to suit any type of fabric and in a seemingly endless array of colours. You will develop your own personal preference for certain kinds of thread, but the general rule is to choose a natural fibre for natural fabrics and a synthetic thread for man-made fabrics. This way, the fabric and thread will have the same characteristics. Having said that, there are now new threads available – for example, cotton-covered polyester – which are just as suitable for both natural and man-made fabrics.

Needles are also important. Most beginners use far too large a needle. You will get much better results if you use a very fine needle for hand sewing. Although you may find it awkward at first, gradually reduce the size of needle you use to a 'betweens' needle, and use a thimble, and you will find hand sewing becomes much easier and faster.

You will also need a tape measure, tailor's chalk and dressmaker's pins. Choose the glass-headed variety of pins – they are sharp, easy to handle and not easily lost.

You are now ready to start on the next stage, cutting out.

LESSON THREE

Cutting out

This is the stage that most home dressmakers approach rather nervously. And this is understandable. You have just bought a pattern you like and hopefully some really good fabric, and it is important that your first venture into dressmaking should be a success to encourage you. So this chapter gives you a step-by-step routine to follow each time you cut out.

Approach the cutting out patiently and methodically and you will become quite engrossed in the job. You will find that this stage is creative and satisfying, resulting in a pile of neatly stacked fabric pieces waiting for more attention. At that stage, leave it and have a well-earned cup of coffee!

A ROUTINE FOR CUTTING OUT

First, turn to your fabric, smooth it flat on a large table and check the following points:

1 Make sure that the ends of the fabric are even. Pin them together and, if necessary, straighten them. If there is no line or pattern on the fabric to guide you in this, snip the selvage and pick up one weft thread with a pin. Pull on this thread gently, easing the fabric along this thread with the other hand. Cut the fabric along this pulled thread and work right across the fabric in this way (Fig 3.1).

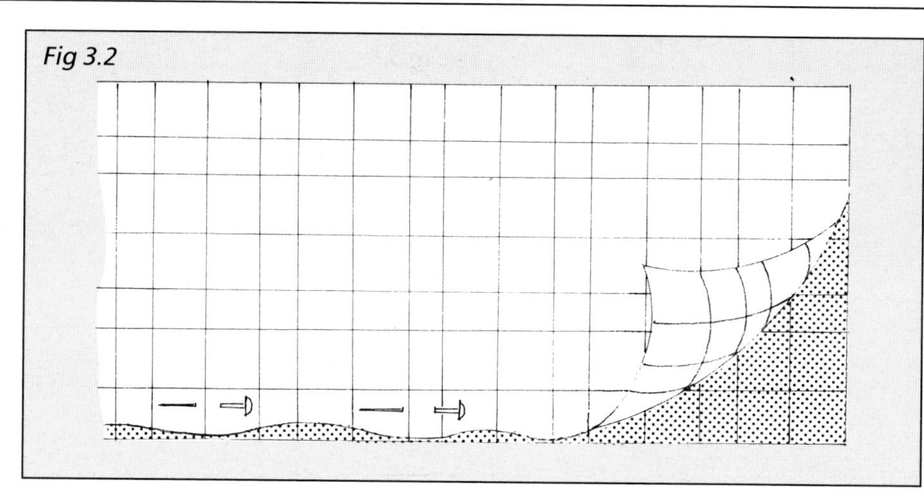

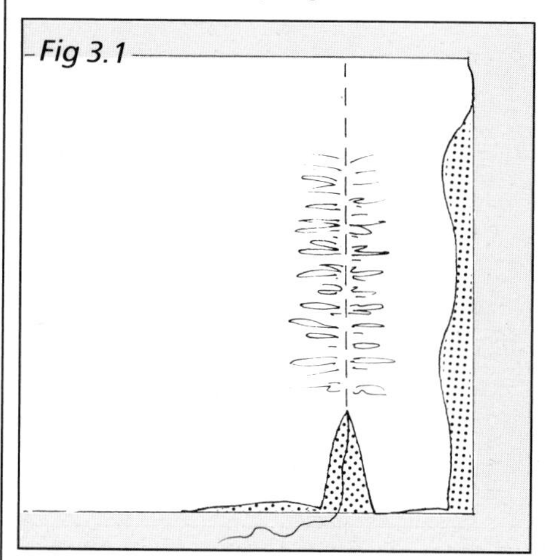

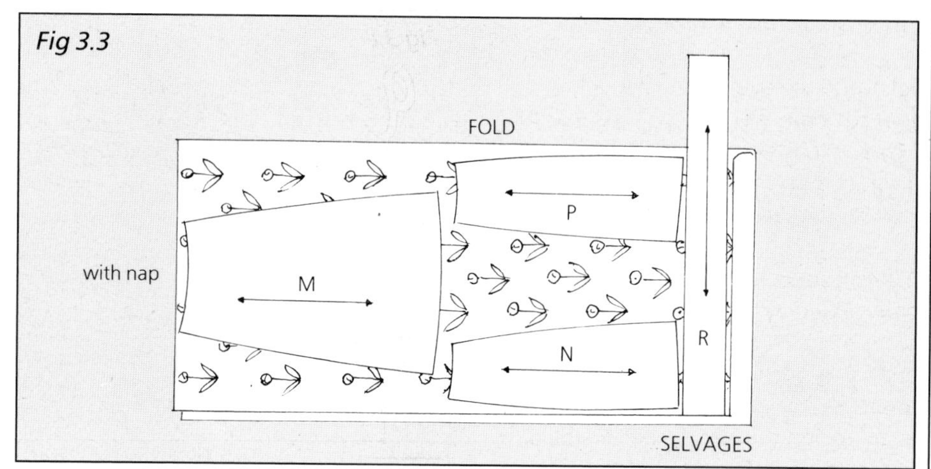

2 Make sure that the selvages of the fabric lie together. Pin them together at intervals. If you are using a checked fabric, pin on the dominant line of each check and make sure that the check of the underneath layer of fabric is identical to the one on top (Fig 3.2).

3 Does the fabric have nap, or a one-way design (see page 14)? If so, make sure that you follow a cutting layout for nap fabrics (Fig 3.3).

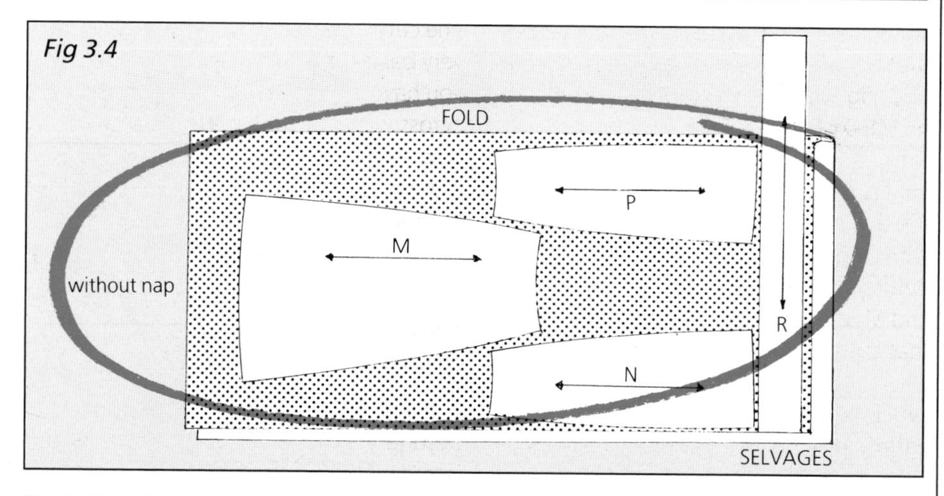

Next, open out your skirt pattern and have a look at the instruction sheet. The first page contains a great deal of helpful information about patterns in general. Take time to read through this.

Below this you will find several cutting layouts for your skirt in different widths. Only one of these layouts applies to you. To find your layout look for the following: the fabric width which is the same as yours, your pattern size, the view of the pattern you are making. Find the cutting layout which relates to these three things and circle it (Fig 3.4). It is a help to mark it as it saves confusion.

Study the relevant cutting layout and check that your fabric is placed on the table in the same way, e.g. with the selvage towards you and the fold of the fabric away from you.

Next, open out the tissue pattern and identify the pieces you need for the view you are making – each piece has a letter to help you identify it – and tick them off as you find them. (This is a good habit to get into because, when you progress to patterns with a large number of pieces, it is easy to overlook the smaller pieces.) Fold the other pieces and put them back into the envelope.

Fig 3.1 Pulling a thread to straighten the ends of a woven fabric.

Fig 3.2 The checks on the underneath layer of fabric should be identical to those on top.

Fig 3.3 A one-way design or nap fabric layout.

Fig 3.4 Circle the skirt cutting layout for easy identification.

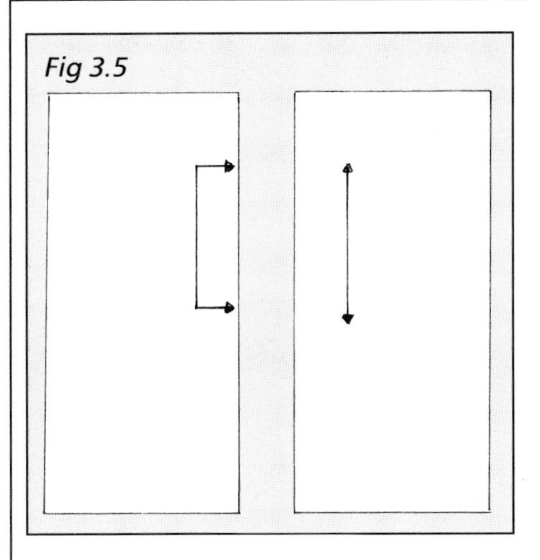
Fig 3.5

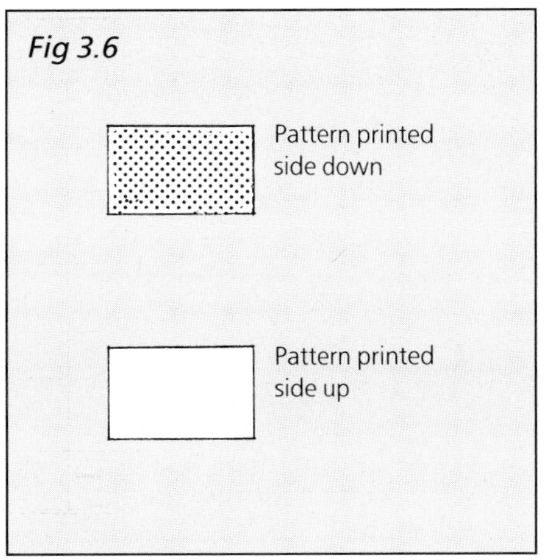

Fig 3.6

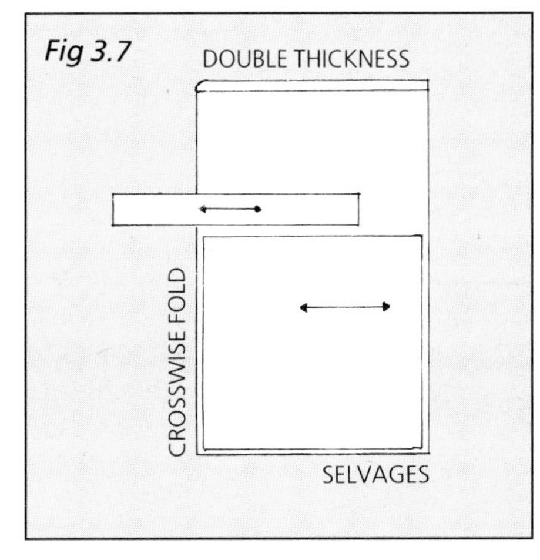

Fig 3.7

PLACING YOUR PATTERN

Following the cutting layout to place out your pattern is a bit like doing a jigsaw. Examine the shape of the piece in the diagram and place it on the fabric in the way shown on the cutting layout.

It does help to have a definite starting point. The best place to start is with the *grain line*, which is the arrow clearly printed on the tissue paper. It takes two forms: it is either fairly central on the tissue, or it is at one edge. In the middle of the tissue, it means 'place this line parallel to the edge of the fabric' (i.e. on the straight grain of the fabric); placed at one edge, it is clearly marked 'place line on FOLD of fabric' (Fig 3.5).

That is where you start. Roughly position the first pattern piece on the fabric and, with a centre arrow, measure the distance between the edge of the fabric and each end of the arrow. Adjust the pattern so that these distances are the same. Pin.

When the arrow indicates that the pattern piece must be placed to the fold, it means *exactly* that. Be accurate – remember that the fabric is double and any discrepancy will be doubled.

When you have positioned these arrows, or, more correctly, grain lines, smooth out the rest of the pattern piece and pin it in place. Put in a pin at each corner and plenty of pins on the curves. Place the pins inside the cutting line (which is indicated by a pair of scissors) and at right angles to it. Continue to place the other pattern pieces in the same way, following the cutting layout.

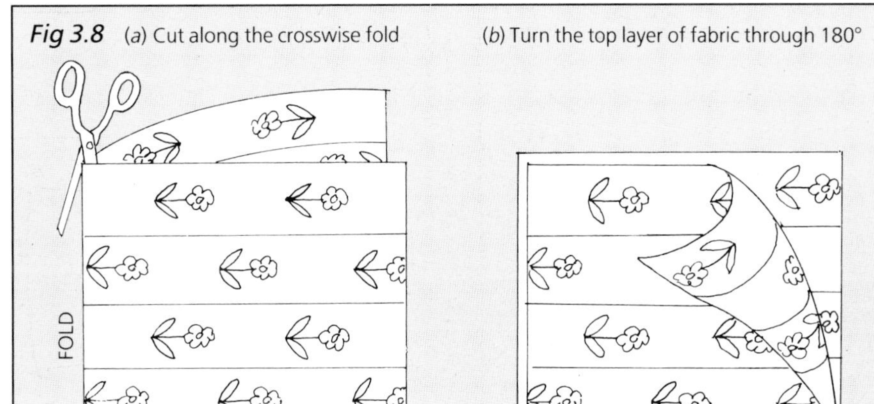

Fig 3.8 (*a*) Cut along the crosswise fold (*b*) Turn the top layer of fabric through 180°

The cutting layout shown in Fig 3.4 is a very basic one. The layout for the pattern you have chosen and those you come across when you go on to make other types of garment may include one or more of the following variations. Watch out for these.

1 Pattern pieces which are shown shaded are reversed; in other words, the printed side of the pattern must be placed face down on the fabric (Fig 3.6).

2 If a pattern piece is shown extending beyond the fold of the fabric in the layout (see Fig 3.7), it means that the fabric has to be opened out and that piece cut from single fabric.

3 If a pattern piece has to be cut out twice from a single layer of fabric, do remember to reverse the pattern the second time you cut. If you don't, you will end up with two left fronts and no right front, for example.

4 Sometimes you will find that, in the cutting layout, the fabric has not been laid with the selvages together, but has been opened out and refolded across the width, as in Fig 3.7. This is because a narrow fabric, such as a 90 cm (36 in) width, when it is folded lengthwise, cannot accommodate the full width of the skirt pattern piece. This is only a problem when you are using a nap or one-way design fabric, where refolding across the width will mean that the pile or the pattern is running one way on the underneath layer and in the opposite direction on the top (Fig 3.8*a*). To rectify this, cut the fabric along the crosswise fold line and turn the top layer through 180° (Fig 3.8*b*).

Fig 3.5 Begin with the arrows denoting the grain lines.

Fig 3.6 Make sure you check which way up your pattern pieces should be placed on the fabric.

Fig 3.7 If a pattern piece extends beyond the fold of the fabric in the layout, open the fabric out and cut that piece from single fabric.

Fig 3.8 The pattern or pile of one-way design or nap fabrics must run the same way on both layers of fabric when crosswise folding is indicated on the cutting layout.

(*continued from page 19*)

5 If a piece has to be cut out twice, you will find the same pattern piece is shown twice on the cutting layout. On the actual tissue, it will state CUT FOUR which, of course, is what you get when you cut twice on the double fabric. It is always worth checking the tissue quickly to see how many times a piece is to be cut. Sometimes, you will find CUT ONE, which means that that piece should be cut on single fabric.

MATCHING CHECKED FABRICS

To look smart, checks should match at all skirt seams and should finish on a suitable check at the hem. The skirt seam lines are joined by matching the notches printed on the paper pattern, so it follows that if you place the appropriate notches on the seam lines on the same check, then the lines of the check will match (Fig 3.9).

It helps to place the notches that you wish to match on a dominant line of the check. Also, turn up the hem allowed on the paper pattern to show you where the checks on the fabric will finish. Move the pattern up or down as necessary. To enable you to do this, extra fabric is usually needed for matching checks. A shaped skirt piece will form an attractive chevron at the side seams. (Remember this only applies to an *even* check fabric – Fig 3.10*a*. Beginners should avoid an *uneven* check – Fig 3.10*b*.)

Most hemlines curve upwards slightly at the side seams. With a check fabric, keep the hemline straight, following the line of the check as indicated by the dotted line in Fig 3.9.

If you look over the list above each time you place on a pattern, then you can cut out more confidently. Cut out with sharp, long-bladed scissors using long strokes. Cut exactly on the marked cutting line, and do not lift the fabric as you cut: keep the scissors on the table and place your left hand flat on top of the fabric alongside the scissors (Fig 3.11).

Always cut the small notches *outwards*, even if on some patterns they are marked inside the cutting line. Cut this way, the notches are much easier to see and they leave the seam allowance intact.

Fig 3.9 Matching checks.

Fig 3.10 Even and uneven checks.

Fig 3.11 Cutting out your pattern pieces.

Fig 3.9

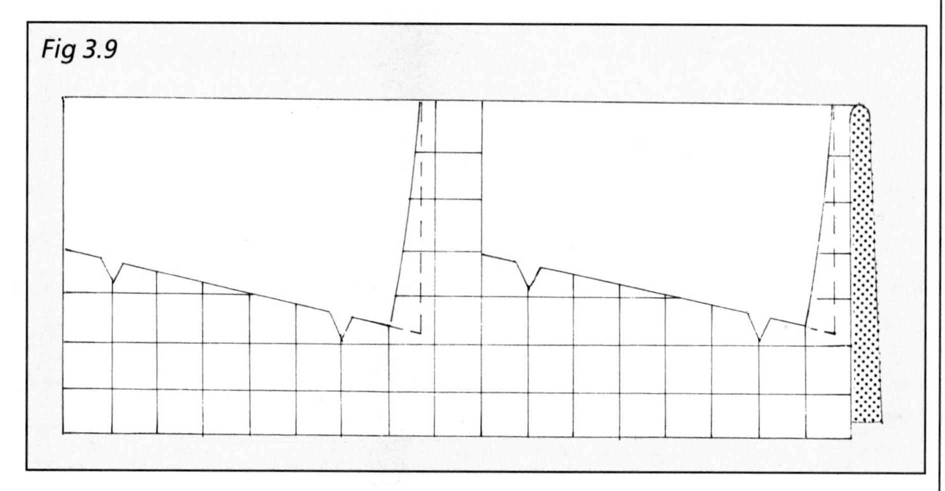

Fig 3.10 (*a*) An even check

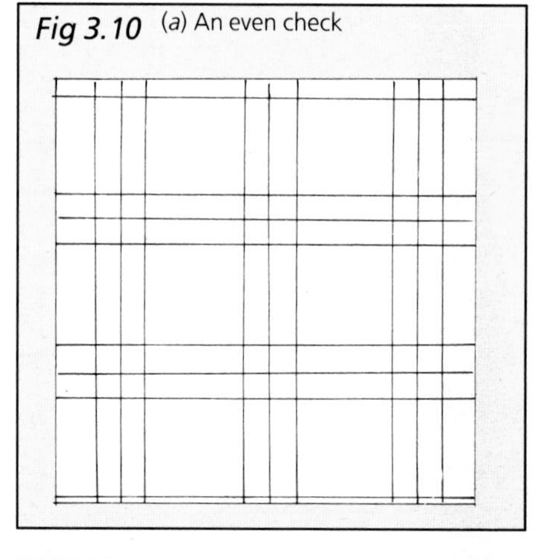

(*b*) An uneven check

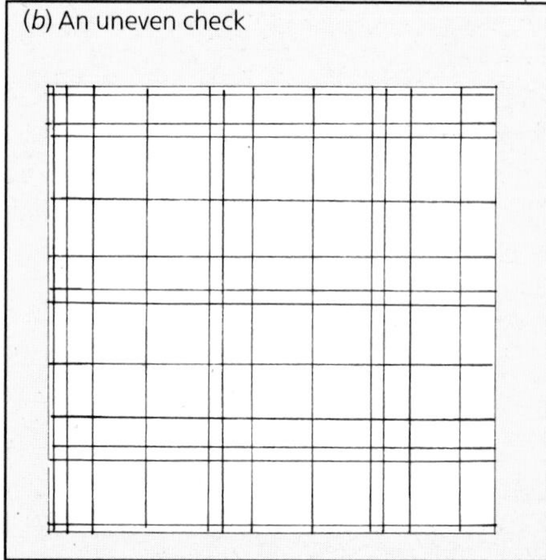

Fig 3.11

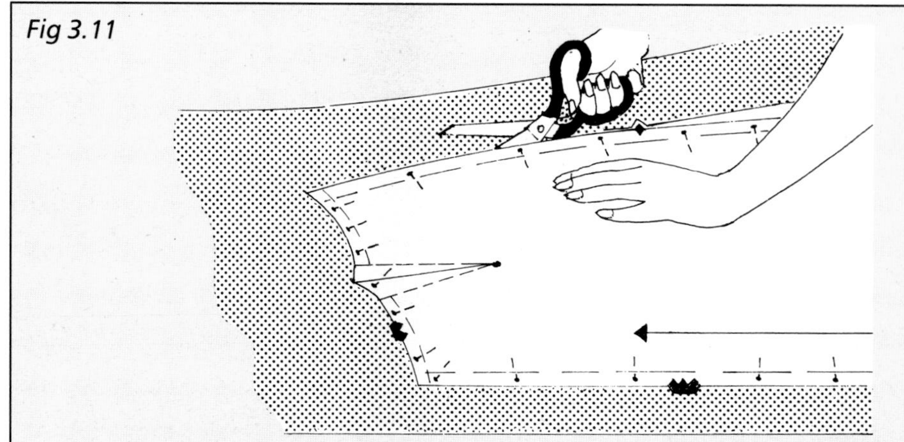

LESSON FOUR

Making your mark

This is the shortest lesson in this dressmaking course, but it is the one which involves the most work! The preparation stages in dressmaking are important, and this next stage, marking your fabric, is *very* important. It will, admittedly, seem a little tedious to you at first, but the time spent now transferring information from your pattern to the fabric will make joining up the pieces *very* much simpler later on.

You need to mark the following:

1 Stitching lines.

2 The centre front line which is usually indicated by a broken line. This is especially important on a blouse or jacket.

3 Darts.

4 The construction symbols. These are small and medium dots.

5 Fold lines, usually indicated by a solid line.

The best way to mark these is with *tailor's tacks*. There *are* quicker ways of marking using carbon or tailor's chalk, and short cuts like snipping your fabric, but these are not the best ways and they often end in a tiresome waste of time when you have to go back and place the pattern on again and refer to it. So it is far better to do the job properly at the outset and make markings with thread.

The *long* lines of stitching can be marked by a quick method of thread marking, the lazy way.

LAZY THREAD MARKING

To do this, use a long double thread and take a small stitch through the pattern and fabric on the line you need to mark. Move on about 5 cm (2 in) and take another small stitch. Continue tacking down the line in this way. Then cut the long stitches in two and gently ease the pattern off the fabric (Fig 4.1). Ease the two layers of fabric apart and snip the threads joining them in half, leaving a tuft of thread on each piece.

Obviously, this tacking is not very secure and you will lose some of the threads, but on long lines of stitching this will not matter as the general line is indicated.

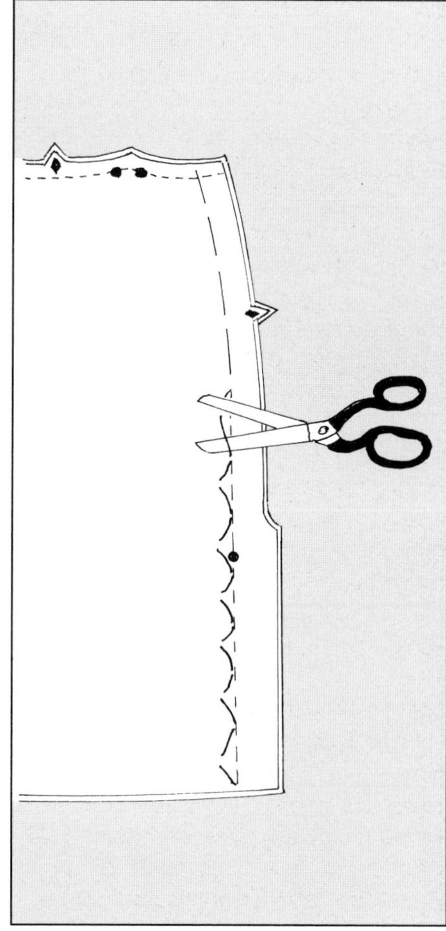

Fig 4.1 Lazy thread marking.

Fig 4.2 Tailor's tacking the correct way.

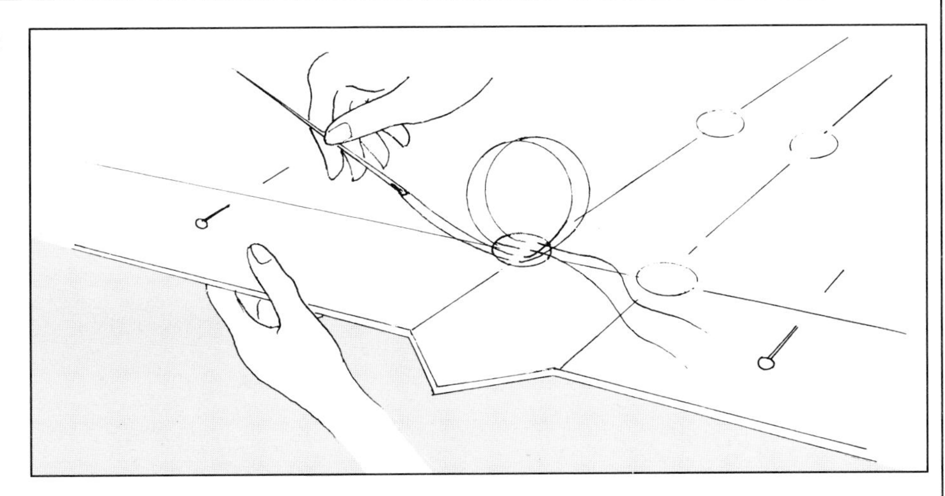

TAILOR'S TACKING*

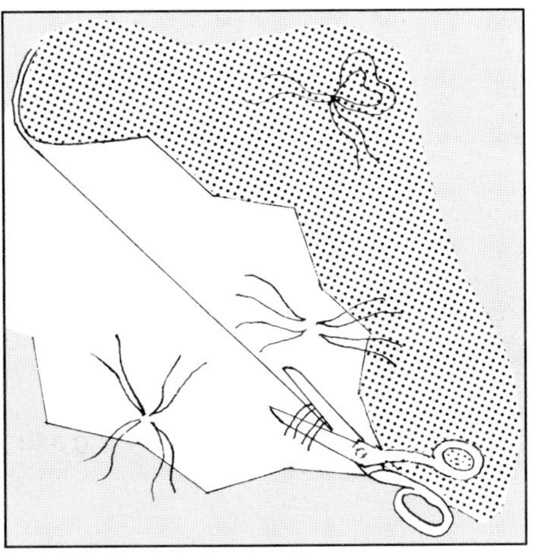

Fig 4.3 Cutting the tailor's tacking threads between the layers of fabric.

The markings where accuracy is very important – for instance, the construction symbols and darts – must be marked with proper tailor's tacking.

To do this, use a long double thread and take a small stitch through the pattern symbol and fabric, leaving an end of about 2.5 cm (1 in). Take a second stitch on top of the first, forming a loop of about 5 cm (2 in). Cut the thread, leaving an end of 2.5 cm (1 in) (Fig 4.2). Gently ease the pattern off the fabric, ease the two layers of fabric apart and cut between them, leaving a tuft of thread on each side (Fig 4.3). Some people prefer to cut the loop rather than make a small tear in the pattern. But if you leave the loop intact, you do not lose the thread mark.

So that your fabric does not become covered with undecipherable thread markings, *use different colours of thread to denote different things.* For example, use white thread for the seam lines, blue for buttonholes and red for the centre lines. It is important when marking pleat lines on a skirt to mark the broken lines in a different colour from the solid lines. Then write on your pattern envelope what each colour signifies.

You will find it worth while to make the following additions when marking your fabric:

1 As you remove each pattern piece, label it. Just pin a small piece of paper on to the fabric with a description of each piece, e.g. 'skirt front', or 'skirt side back', or 'bodice back'. The pieces can be very confusing once the pattern is removed.
2 If your fabric looks very similar on the right and the wrong sides, mark the wrong side either with a bold chalk mark or, again, with a slip of paper.

3 Go over the tailor's tacking lines marking the centre front of the garment with a long line of brightly coloured double thread. If you are using a pile fabric such as corduroy, put an arrow in chalk indicating the way of the pile on any small pieces you are likely to stitch upside down by mistake, e.g. patch pockets.

Once you have finished the thread marking, and if you are the methodical type, return your pattern pieces to the envelope, neatly folded and in alphabetical order, so that, should you need to refer to a pattern piece again, you can identify it by letter from the pattern primer and select it at once from your envelope.
Now, with a neat stack of fabric pieces, thread marked and clearly labelled, you are ready for the next stage.

*'Tailor's tacking' = Basting.

LESSON FIVE

Putting in the zip

Putting in the zip?! Yes, because you are making a skirt, this really *is* the next lesson. With one exception: if you have chosen a pattern with a side zip, you will have to skip this chapter and return to it after you have completed Lesson Six.

As most skirts nowadays are designed with the zip at the centre back, the easiest thing to do is to put in the zip first, that is, before the side seams are tacked up and you try on the garment for fitting. Any alteration that you need to make will be made at the side seams. So you can safely join the centre back skirt seam and then work with the skirt back pieces flat on the table, which makes things much easier.

First, stitch the centre back seam up as far as the mark for the zip, leaving the rest of the seam open. (Read through the parts of Lesson Six on 'Starting to sew', and 'Pressing' (page 34) before you do this.)

Fig 5.1 Turn back and tack the seam turnings.

Fig 5.2 Pin and tack the zip.

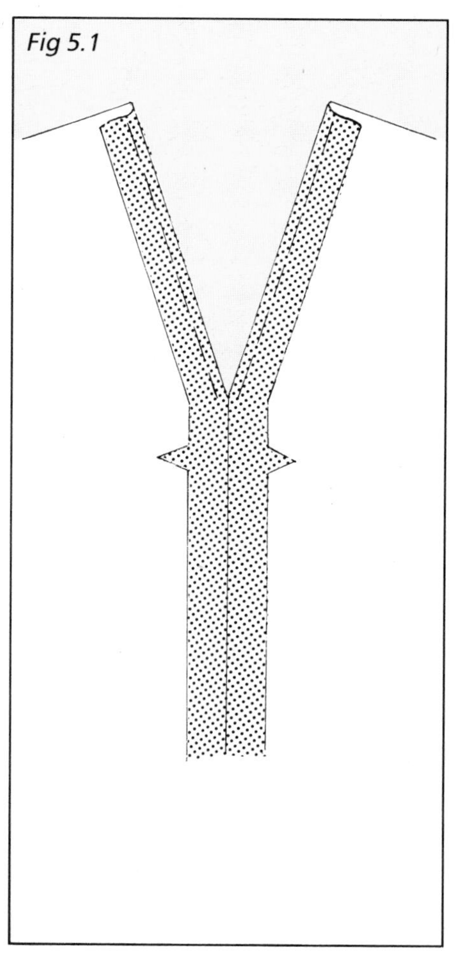

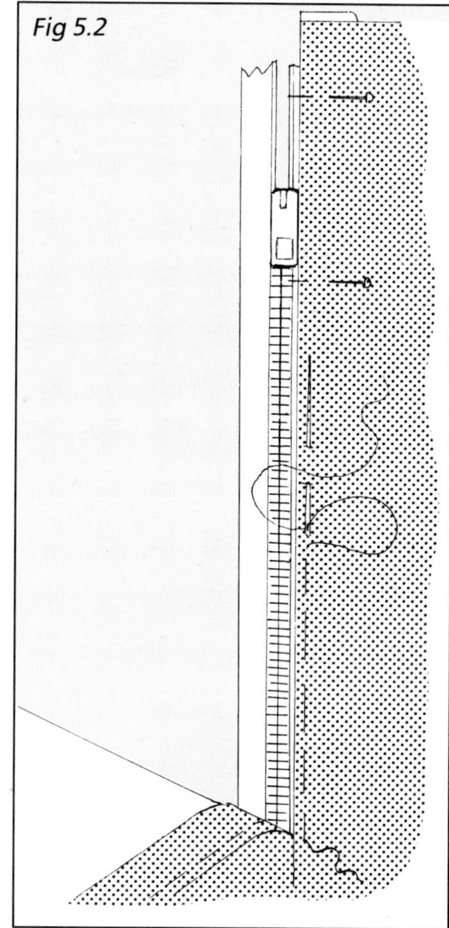

AN EASY METHOD FOR INSERTING A CONCEALED ZIP

If you are a complete beginner at dressmaking, or have never put in a zip to your own satisfaction, follow this method of zip insertion *exactly*. It is neat and unobtrusive and will give you good results every time.

1 Turn back to the wrong side the correct seam allowance on both sides above the notch marking the position for the zip. Tack down the folded edges and press them (Fig 5.1).

2 Place the skirt back flat on the table, right side uppermost. Position the zip with the zip pull at the top, so that the edge of the teeth is against the fold of the fabric on the right-hand side of the seam, and the zip pull is 6 mm (1/4 in) down from the stitching line for the waistband. Tack the zip in position (Fig 5.2).

3 Exchange the usual foot on your machine for the zipper foot. (A zipper foot has only one side to it so that the machine needle can stitch very close to the teeth of the zip. All machines are equipped with one and changing the feet is a simple matter. (Refer to your machine manual if you are in doubt.) Starting at the base of the zip, stitch down the fold as close to the edge as you can (Fig 5.3).

4 Bring the other side of the zip opening over to conceal the zip completely, with the folded edge lying on top of the line of machine stitching. (The edges will overlap just a fraction at this stage.) Tack the folded edge in place securely, using short diagonal tacking stitches (Fig 5.4).

5 The zip has now to be top-stitched. To make sure that you get this line of stitching straight, it is a good idea to give yourself a guideline to follow: make a line of small tacking stitches in a contrast colour of thread parallel to the folded edge and 9 mm (3/8 in) away from it (Fig 5.5).

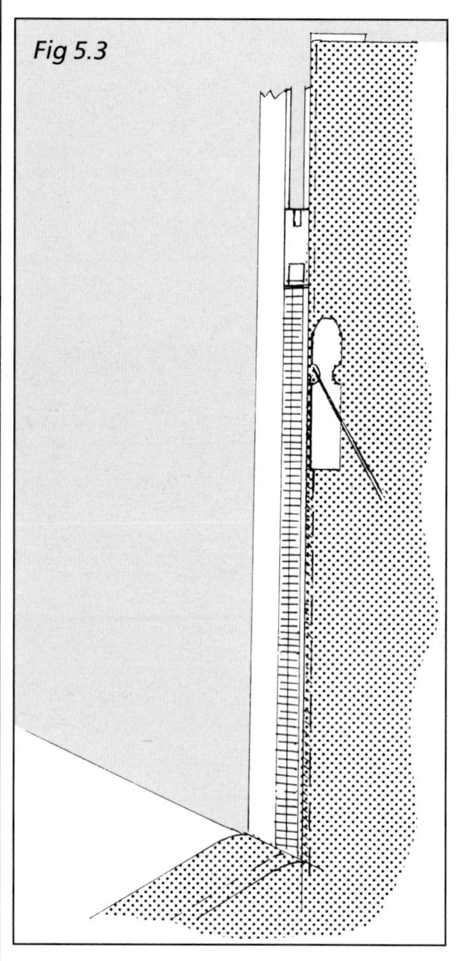

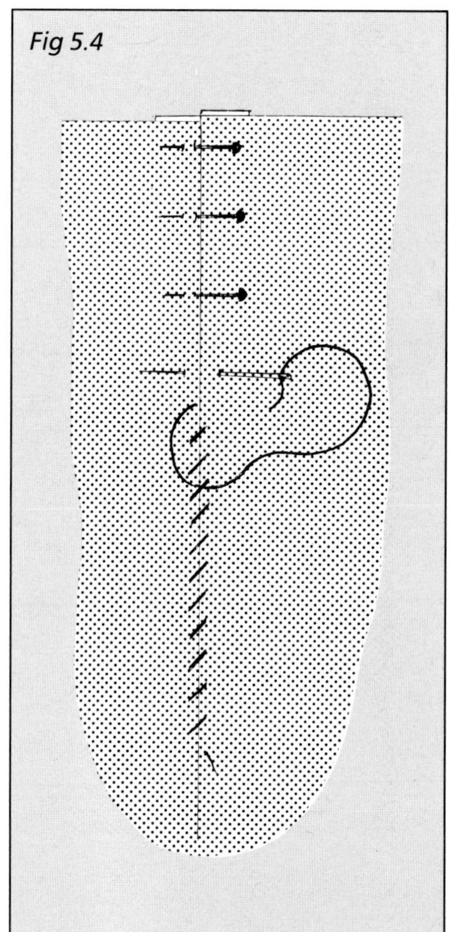

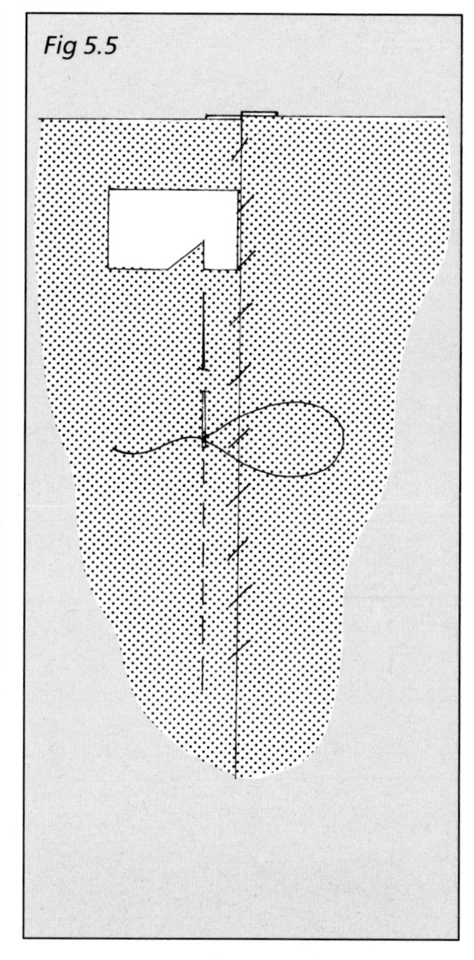

Fig 5.3 Stitch the folded edge.

Fig 5.4 Tack the folded edges together over the zip teeth.

Fig 5.5 Tack along the guideline.

6 Using the zipper foot, stitch the zip, following the guideline, and stitch across the end of the zip at an angle (Fig 5.6). Remove the tacking and guideline and press the zip.

When you have put in several zips following this method, you will find it fairly quick and easy. You can either stick to this method, or you might like to try a slight variation, putting the first line of stitching to the *inside* of the seam so that it is hidden, and putting in the top line of stitching by hand.

INSERTING A ZIP BY HAND

1 Fold back the correct seam allowance on the left-hand side of the skirt back only. On the right-hand side, mark the seam line with a line of tacking stitches.

2 Place the skirt back flat on a table, wrong side uppermost. Place the zip with the zip pull facing *downwards* on the right-hand seam allowance and the edge of the teeth next to the line of tacking. Make sure that the zip pull is 6 mm (¼ in) down from the waist stitching line as before. Tack in place.

3 Stitch, using the zipper foot on the machine, as close to the teeth as possible, from the stop at the bottom of the zip tape to the end of the tape at the top (Fig 5.7).

4 Turn the zip to the right side and tack back the seam turning on that edge. Bring the other side of the zip opening over to close the seam and completely conceal the zip. Tack securely with diagonal tacking stitches.

5 Follow stage 5 opposite.

6 Complete the top-stitching of the zip by hand, using a stab stitch, which is similar to a back stitch but the stitches are not joined. Use a good colour match of thread and a very small needle. Bring the needle through to the right side. Take a stitch back for just a thread or two (the smallest stitch you can make), taking up the thickness of the fabric and the zip tape. Bring the needle out just in front of the thread (Fig 5.8). The stitches become small dots and are virtually invisible.

With the zip inserted successfully, you are ready to start joining up the skirt pieces to give yourself some idea of what the finished skirt will look like.

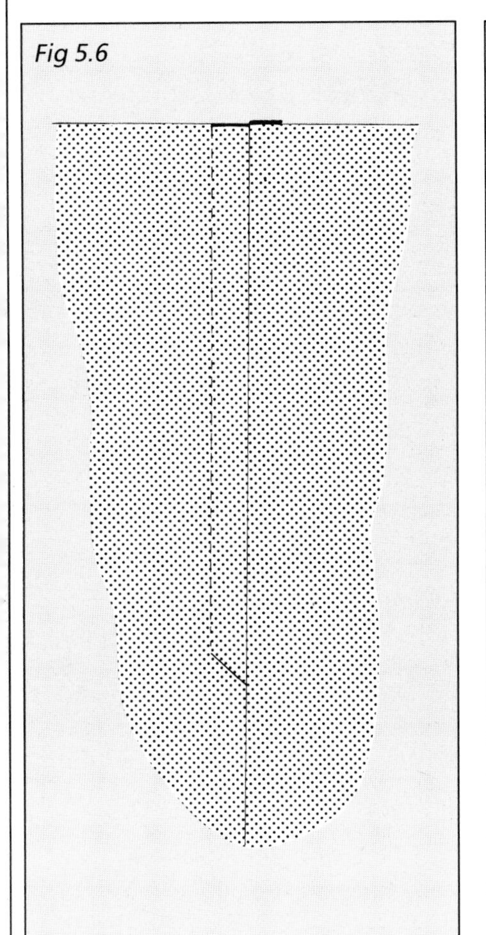

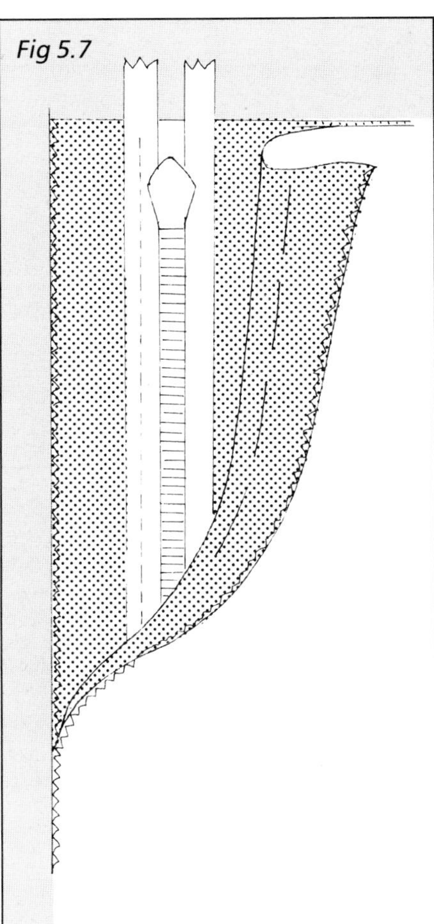

Fig 5.6 Stitch the zip.

Fig 5.7 Stitch as close to the zip teeth as possible.

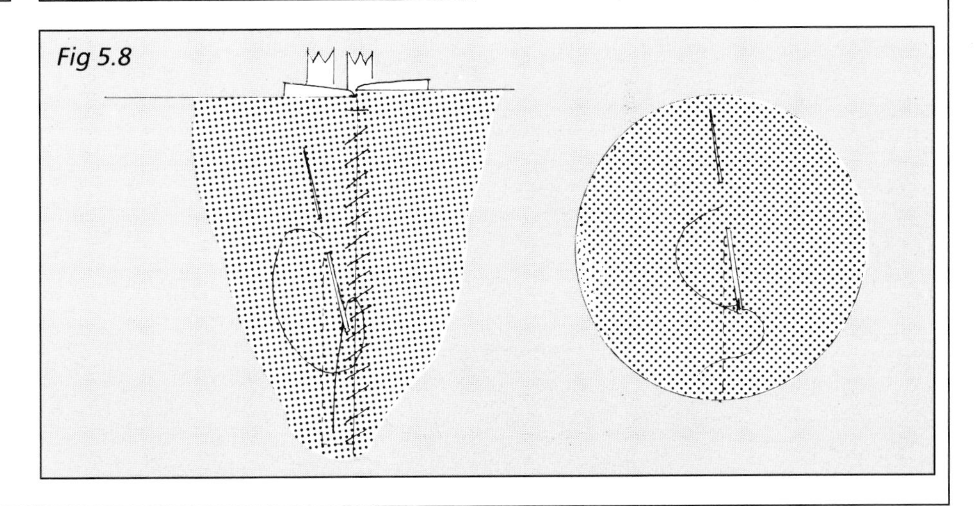

Fig 5.8 Bring out the needle just in front of the thread.

LESSON SIX

Getting it together

You are now at a most interesting stage in making up your skirt – tacking it together to try it on. Your pattern primer (i.e. the instruction sheet) will give you the order in which to tack up the separate pieces, so refer to it and keep to the order it suggests.

Place the fabric pieces on a table. *Always* work with the pieces flat and never on your knee. Place the cut edges of the seams together, matching the notches. Pin, with the pins at right angles to the edges.

Working from right to left and starting with a large knot in the thread, tack down the long seams. Use a long-and-short stitch, making the long stitch about 2.5 cm (1 in) and the short stitch 6 mm (¼ in) (Fig 6.1). Finish the seam with a secure backstitch.

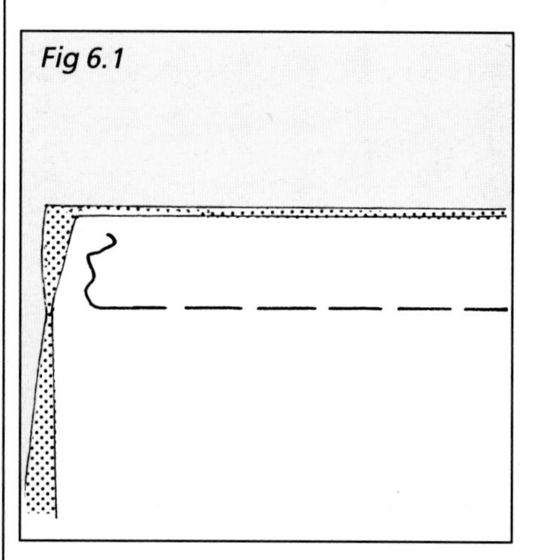

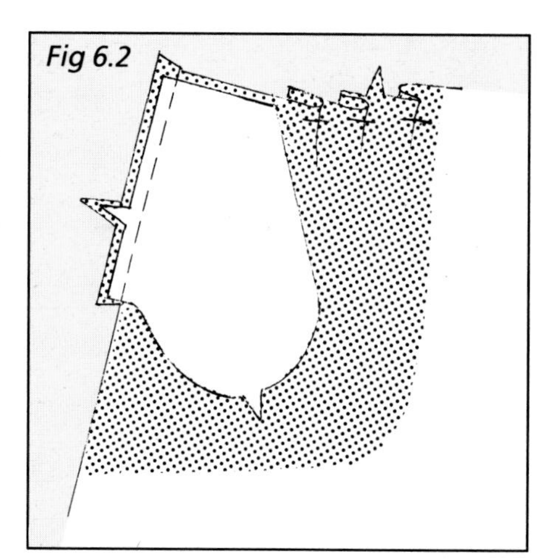

SKIRT POCKETS

Many skirt patterns have pockets set into the side seam, and this will usually be the first unit your pattern instructions will deal with. For a beginner, this looks like a complicated procedure, but, in fact, it is fairly simple and straightforward.

The side seams have an extension, i.e. the side seams are wider where the pockets have to go. Place the small curved pocket pieces, right sides together to the seam extensions, on the skirt front and back, matching the notches and thread marks. Tack and stitch (Fig 6.2). Press these seams open.

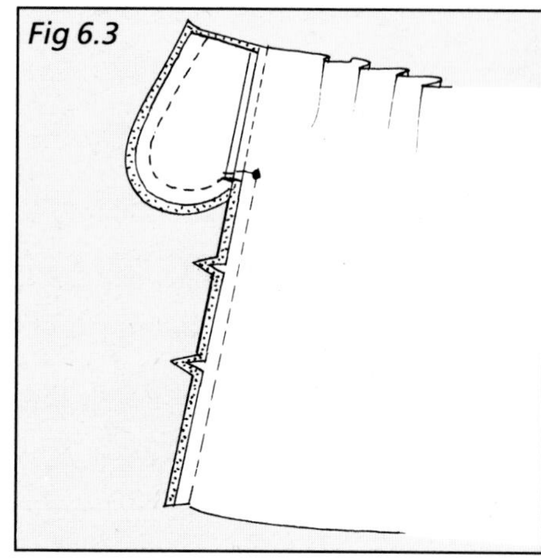

Pin the skirt front to the back at the side seams, matching the notches in the side seams and the thread marks in the pocket extension. (These will be the large dots on the paper pattern.) Tack and stitch down the side seam, pivoting the fabric, with the needle still in the work, at the thread marks, to stitch round the pockets and continue down the rest of the seam (Fig 6.3).

Fig 6.1 Long-and-short stitches for tacking.

Fig 6.2 Stitch the pocket to the seam extension.

Fig 6.3 Stitch round the pocket, pivot at the mark and continue down the seam.

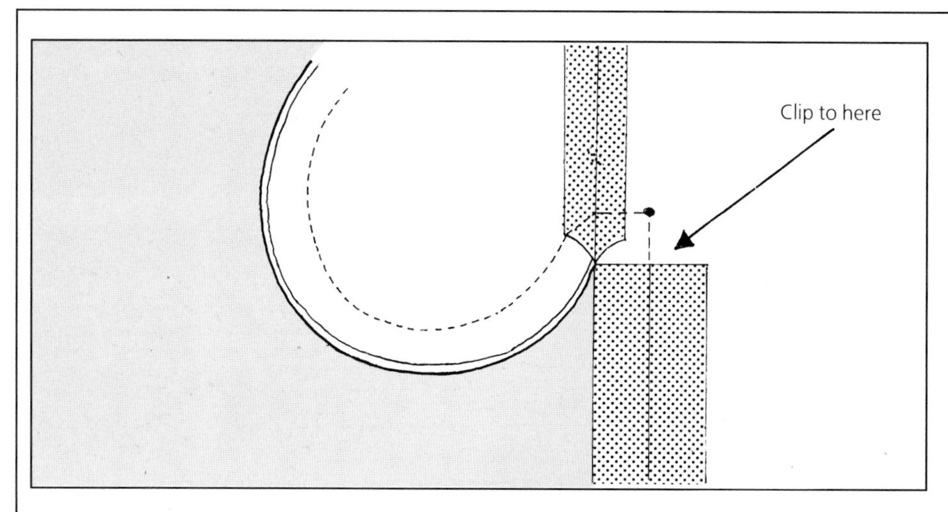

Fig 6.4 Clip the fabric almost to the stitching line.

Fig 6.5 Pleats.

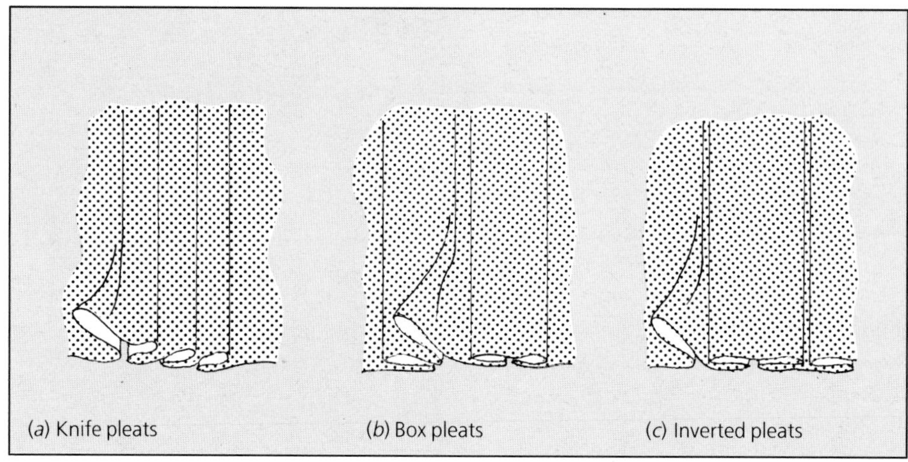

Press the seam open as far as you can. When you do this, it will become obvious that, in fact, you cannot press the seam open at the pocket, without clipping the fabric to the seam line on the back extension. Clip the fabric almost to the stitching line at the thread mark (Fig 6.4). Continue to press the seam, and then press the pocket towards the front.

Patch pockets are sometimes a feature on cotton summer skirts. These are best put on at the end, when the skirt length has been decided, so that you can find the best position for the pocket. For a simple pocket or a self-lined pocket, see pages 46–7.

PLEATS, DARTS AND GATHERS

Dealing with pleats

Pleats are an attractive way of adding fullness to a skirt. The basic pleats are knife pleats, box pleats and inverted pleats (Fig 6.5), with many variations on the way that these types are used in a skirt to get different effects. All pleats need a firmly woven fabric and should be carefully cut on the true grain of the fabric. All types of pleat are dealt with in the same way.

Smooth the fabric flat on a large table, right side uppermost. It is important to mark the pleat lines accurately, so that the pleats will hang straight. As you have followed the instructions in Lesson Four carefully, you now have the pleat lines clearly marked! Lap the fold lines to the broken lines, making sure that the upper edges remain even. Pin and then tack down each pleat using a diagonal tacking (Fig 6.6).

Next, tack through all the thicknesses at the waist edge, with diagonal tacking, to hold the pleats securely (Fig 6.7).

Fig 6.6

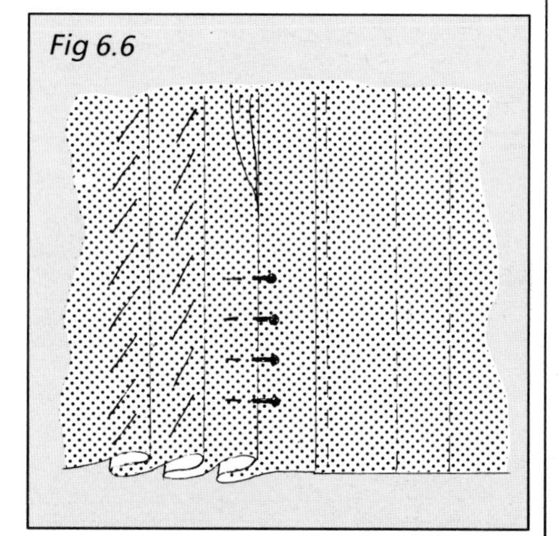

Fig 6.7

Fig 6.6 Tack down the pleat with diagonal tacking.

Fig 6.7 Tack through all thicknesses at the waist.

Press the pleats at this stage. Place the skirt flat along the length of the ironing board; never drape it over the edge. Use a hot iron and a damp cloth and an *up* and *down* movement (see 'Pressing' on page 34). Use considerable pressure, but avoid the hem area. Then press again with a dry cloth and do not move the fabric until all the steam has evaporated and you are sure that the fabric is dry. Do not remove the tacking holding the pleats until the skirt is finished.

If the pleats are to be stitched down part of their length, this is most easily and neatly done at this stage, before the side seams are joined. The stitching can be done with a matching thread to make it inconspicuous, or with another coloured thread to give bold top-stitching (see page 70).

It is often a good idea to stitch the very edge of the pleat on the *inside*, where the stitching will not show but where it will hold the shape of the pleat. This must always be done after pressing and after the hem is turned up. Pleats need careful attention at the hem (see page 44).

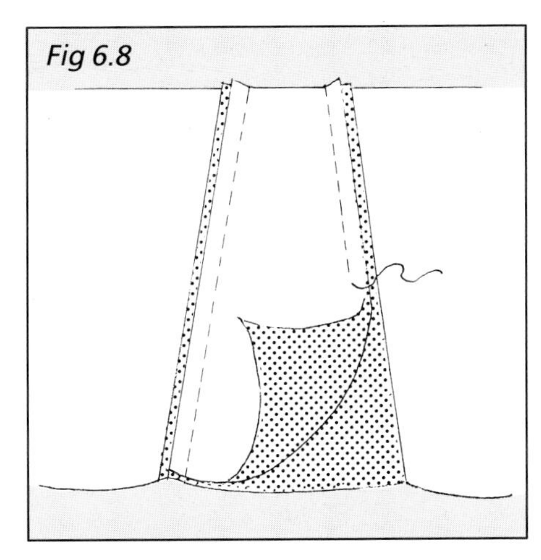

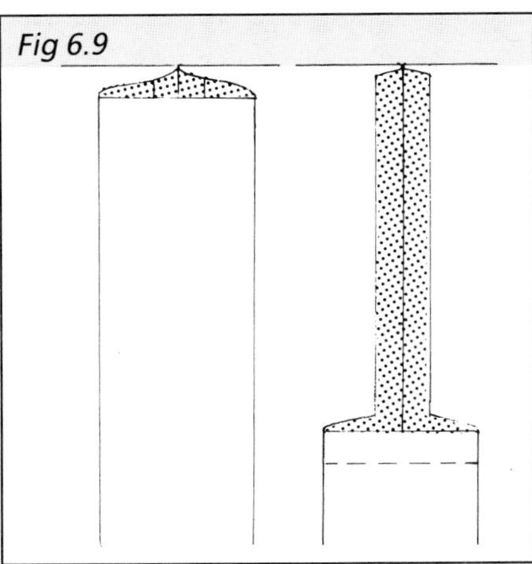

An *inverted pleat* is popular at the centre front or back of a skirt and often has a separate pattern piece for a *pleat underlay*. The seam is stitched part-way down its length, and tacked the rest of the way. The seam is then pressed open and the pleat underlay placed over the opened seam and stitched down the outside edges. When the tacking is removed, this releases the pleat (Fig 6.8).

An inverted pleat without a separate pleat underlay is a simple matter of folding the fabric to form a pleat. Fold the fabric, right sides together on the solid line, matching the broken lines. Stitch to where marked. Open out the fabric so that the stitched line lies on top of the solid line (Fig 6.9).

Fig 6.8 An inverted pleat with a separate pleat underlay.

Fig 6.9 An inverted pleat without a separate pleat underlay.

Fig 6.10 Dealing with darts.

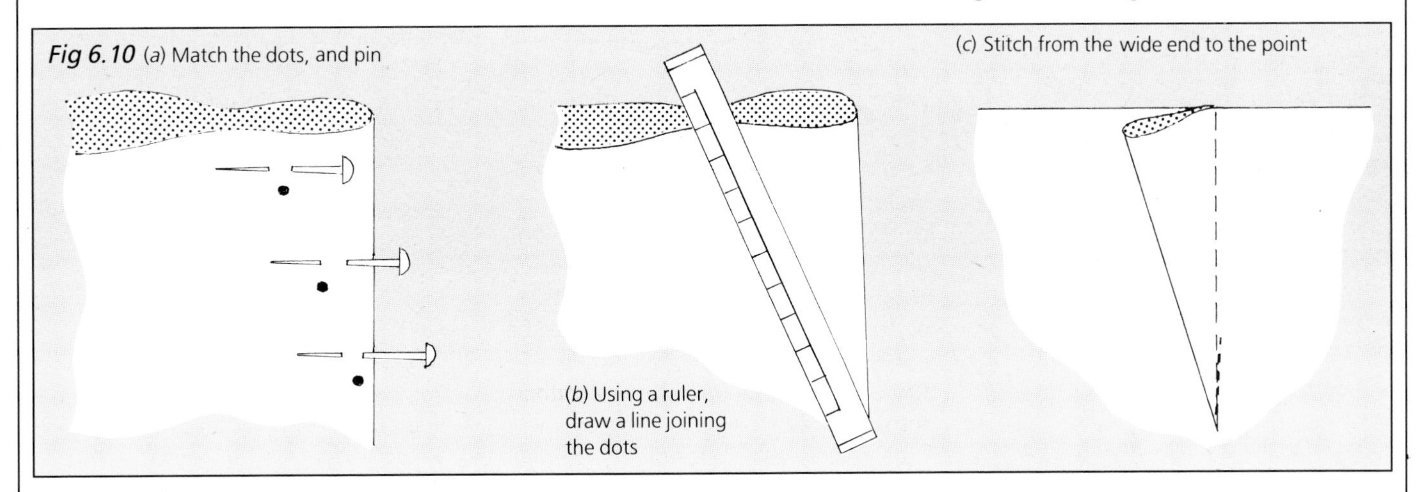

Dealing with darts

A slim-fitting skirt usually has darts at the waistline to shape it over the curve of the hip. With the wrong side of the fabric towards you, pick up the dart, matching the dots. Pin (see Fig 6.10*a*). Now lay the fabric flat on the table with the dart folded to the outside and, using a ruler, chalk a line joining up the dots (Fig 6.10*b*). Tack on this line, tapering to a fine point. Stitch from the wide end of the dart to the point (Fig 6.10*c*). Skirt darts are pressed towards the centre of the skirt.

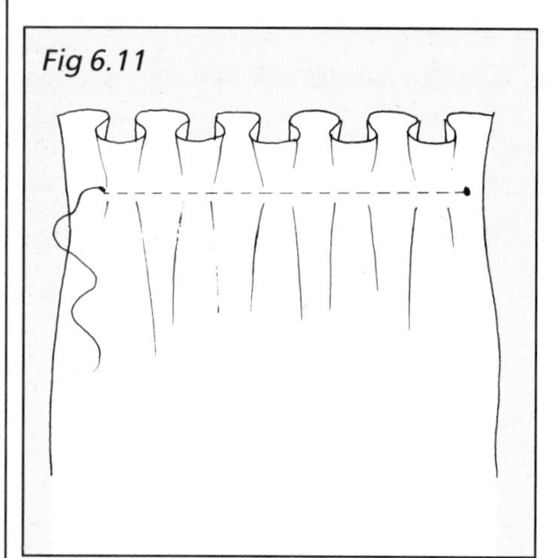

Fig 6.11

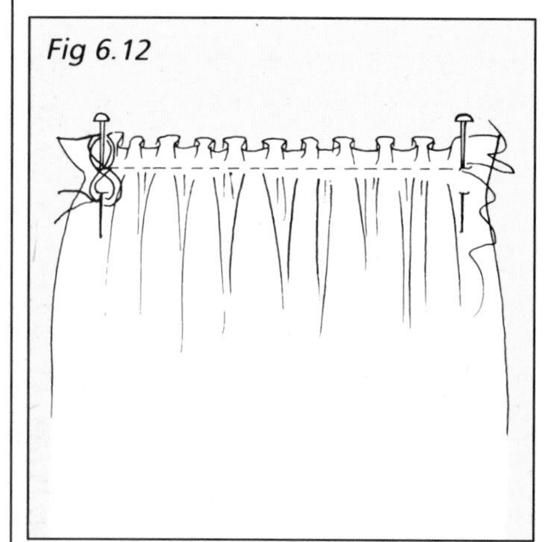

Fig 6.12

Dealing with gathers
A skirt gathered into a waistband is the easiest skirt to make, but it is important that the fullness is evenly distributed and not bunched. A pattern usually suggests working two rows of gathering stitches to draw up the fullness. In practice, by far the easiest way is to work *one* row of gathering in a strong thread. Use a long, strong, single thread and work tiny stitches, by hand, *on or just a fraction above* the actual seamline. This way, the fullness can be handled easily and controlled where you need it.

Start the gathering thread with a large knot. Draw the fabric along the thread, forming gathers. Pull it up by the required amount, then adjust the gathers and distribute them evenly, making sure there are no bunches of gathers and no flat areas. You can check this by holding the work horizontally and looking into the gathered end: the fullness should be in even curves (Fig 6.11). When the gathers are drawn up and adjusted, wrap the end of the thread round a pin to hold it (Fig 6.12).

FITTING

When you have assembled the skirt pieces, it is time to try the skirt on.

Making things fit is basic to good dressmaking and cannot be learned from a book. Fitting is largely a matter of practice and trial and error. Successful sewing depends largely on choosing your correct pattern size, as was explained in Lesson One, so that any alterations to your skirt at this stage are minor. But there are several points to check. (Do not pay any attention to the hemline at this stage; this is levelled once the waistband has been attached.)

The waist Is it a neat and comfortable fit? If you need to reduce it slightly or let it out a little, this should be done at the side seams or by adjusting the darts or the amount of fullness in the gathers.

The hip Is the skirt falling gracefully over the hip? If it is a slim-fitting skirt, is there enough ease so that the skirt is not pulling across the stomach, or riding up to form a fold across the back waist? Make any alteration at the side seams and continue the new line down to the hem. You cannot reduce or let out the skirt at the hip only. The new line should taper to nothing at the waist, curve over the hip and continue parallel to the side seam to the hem.

Fig 6.11 The fullness of gathers should be drawn up in even curves.

Fig 6.12 When you have adjusted the gathers, wrap the thread round a pin to hold it.

STARTING TO SEW

You are now ready to machine-stitch the long seams. Use a thread suitable for the fabric you are working with. There are threads for natural fabrics, special threads for man-made fabrics and threads which suit mixed-fibre fabrics. If in any doubt, ask your retailer for the best thread for your fabric.

A good machine stitch length for general use is 10 to 15 stitches per 2.5 cm (1 in). Always make sure that the thread take-up lever is in its highest position before you start to sew, so that the needle does not unthread. (It is a good habit to leave your sewing machine with the take-up lever in this position by turning the balance wheel *towards* you, never away from you.) Pull the needle and bobbin threads towards the back behind the presser foot, so that they do not get tangled when you start to sew.

Keep the bulk of the fabric on the left as you stitch, and the seam allowance to the right of the presser foot.

The two layers of fabric should feed evenly and smoothly under the presser foot together. If the foot is pushing the top layer into a slight fullness, too much pressure is being exerted by the foot on to the fabric. Your machine has a pressure knob to adjust this. This is particularly useful with thick fabrics.

It is not always necessary to start and end a seam with a reverse stitch, although many people prefer to do so. If the seam line is going to be crossed by another line of stitching, it is obviously going to be held anyway. But it is a good idea to use a reverse stitch at a waistline edge, a neck edge and an armhole edge, where the seams tend to pull apart at the fitting stage.

PRESSING

Whenever you have stitched a seam, or a series of seams, you must *press* them. 'When you stitch it, press it' is the golden rule. It really is *very* important to press as you go along. It makes all the difference to the end product. And you will find it very satisfying as your garment goes together with well-pressed, tailored edges and gradually achieves a professional look. A steam iron is essential for dressmaking, and most fabrics are improved with a damp cloth as well. Pressing is done with an up and down movement – it's *not* ironing!

Before pressing any of your garment, test the iron and the amount of pressure you will need to exert to get a good result on a scrap of your fabric. In general, firmly woven wool and wool mixtures require very heavy pressing with a steam iron and a damp cloth, especially on pleats. Before you move the fabric, dry it off by pressing again with a dry cloth to avoid stretching the wool. Lightweight wools, jerseys and man-made fibres require lighter pressing, using a steam iron and a dry cloth. Cotton, linen and mixtures of natural fibres and polyester cottons can be pressed directly with a steam iron only.

To help you with pressing your fabric, make yourself a *seam roll* – you will find it invaluable. Ask at your fabric shop for the inside cardboard tube from a roll of fabric. Cut it to about 90 cm (36 in) in length, cover it with a layer of old blanket or foam, and then cover that with a piece of old sheet or curtain lining (Fig 6.13). A seam roll is ideal for pressing the long seams on skirts and trousers because, when you position the seam lengthwise over the roll, you press only the stitching line and not the seam turning on either side. This is a boon for navy blue and black fabrics, which glaze readily with an imprint of the seam turnings if pressed badly.

A *tailor's ham* is also useful, though less so than the seam roll. Cut two oval 'ham-shaped' pieces of fabric, 25 cm (10 in) long and about 18 cm (7 in) at the widest point (Fig 6.14). Stitch the pieces together round the outside edges, leaving an opening. Turn the pieces inside out through the opening, and stuff very firmly with polyester filling to obtain a smoothly rounded shape. Oversew the opening together. The ham is ideal for pressing curved seams, darts and the back of a collar.

With your skirt seams stitched and pressed you are ready to add the waistband.

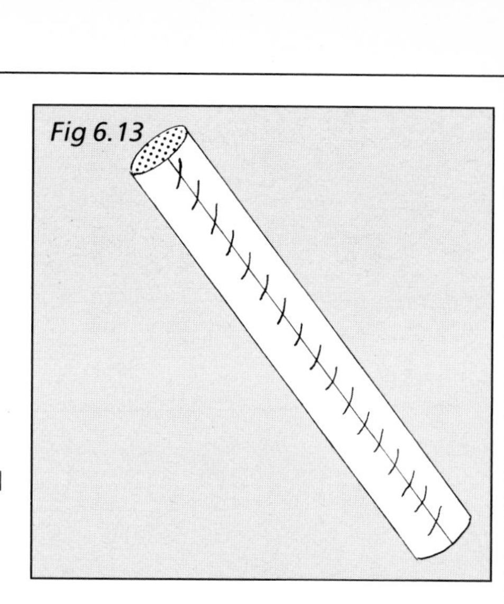

Fig 6.13 A seam roll.

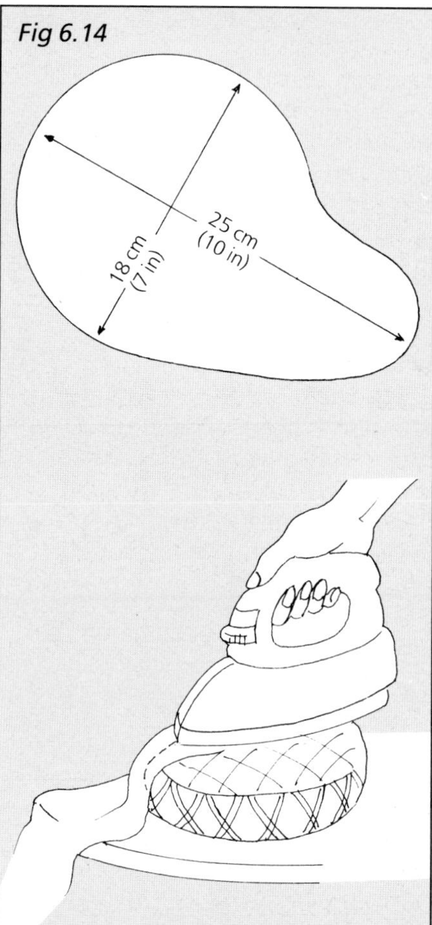

Fig 6.14 A tailor's ham.

LESSON SEVEN

The waistband

One of the many advantages of making your own clothes is that you can get snugly fitting, comfortable waistbands. The best approach is to make the waistband fit *you*, and then make the skirt fit the waistband. It is also easier to leave the stitching of the ends of the band until you have attached it at the waist and tried on the skirt to check the fit and the overlap at each end.

When cutting out a waistband, it is often a good idea to leave extra fabric at each end, even though you have checked your waist against the pattern and altered accordingly. Waist measurements can fluctuate and are not easy to assess until the fitting stage. The extra fabric can be left on as an extra overlap and is there if you ever need to let out the skirt at a later date.

WAISTBAND INTERFACINGS

A skirt waistband has to be interfaced, that is stiffened, to fit snugly and to prevent it stretching or rolling over. There are several excellent ways of doing this. One way is with petersham (straight or curved) and even stretch petersham is now available. Strips of sew-in or iron-on interfacing, cut to size and of a suitable weight, can also be used.

But if you are new to sewing, make it easy for yourself and buy an iron-on waistband interfacing which has perforations marking the stitching and fold lines (Fig 7.1). This makes it very easy to get your stitching lines straight and the width of the waistband exact.

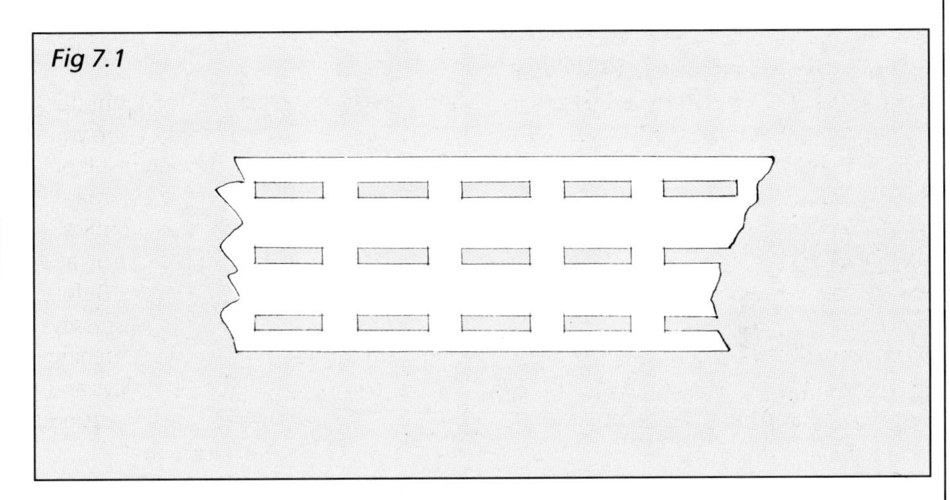

Fig 7.1 Perforated waistband interfacing makes it easy to get stitching lines straight.

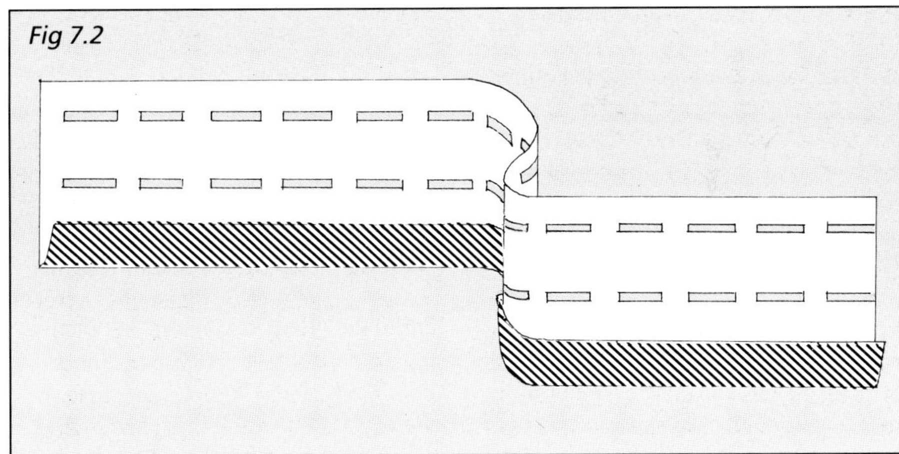

Fig 7.2 Press under the seam allowance down one long side.

Interfacing the band

Centre the interfacing, sticky side down, on the wrong side of the waistband fabric. Press heavily using a damp cloth and a hot iron to ensure a good bond. Fold in half and press along the fold line. Turn under the seam allowance down one long side and press (Fig 7.2).

Attaching the band

Keep the skirt right side out. Place the raw edge of the band to the waistline of the skirt, matching the notches and allowing an overlap at one end as indicated in your pattern. Tack firmly along the waist stitching line and then try on the skirt to check that the waist fits snugly, as this is the stage to adjust the fit if necessary.

If the skirt needs to be taken in, or let out a little, this can be done at the side seams (the adjustment is divided equally between the two seams), the darts, or any gathered sections.

If you want to add loops to hang up your skirt, they are put into the waistband at this stage. Cut two lengths of seam binding or ribbon about 10 cm (4 in) long. Fold them in half and insert the ends into the waist stitching line, one at each side seam (Fig 7.3).

Machine-stitch the waistband to the skirt at the waist stitching line. Trim the seam to 6 mm (¼ in).

Stitching the ends

One end of the band is sewn in line with the skirt edge and the other is left projecting as overlap. It is neater to have the overlap on the underneath of the band, i.e. on the skirt back.

Fold the ends of the band on the fold line, right side to the inside. Stitch across the ends (Fig 7.4). Trim the seam and cut off the corners. Tùrn the ends right side out. Press.

Bring the long folded edge of the band down on to the stitching line and hem in place, oversewing the open edges of the overlap together (Fig 7.5).

Using petersham

To use petersham or sew-in interfacing instead of iron-on to stiffen your waistband, the procedure is the same, but to hold it in place, either invisibly catch-stitch the petersham to the fabric band (Fig 7.6*a*) or machine-stitch it to the fabric on the inner side of the band (Fig 7.6*b*).

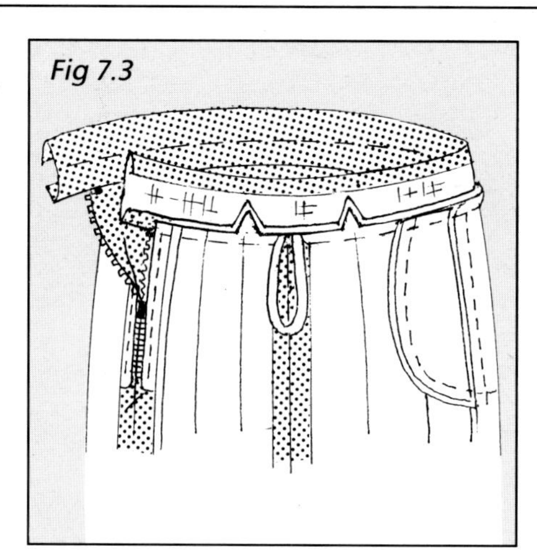

Fig 7.3 Insert ribbon loops into waist stitching at side seams.

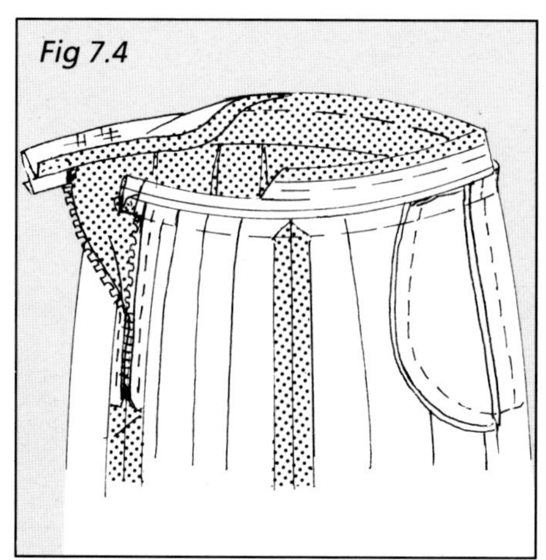

Fig 7.4 Fold the ends of the bands, right sides together, and stitch across the ends.

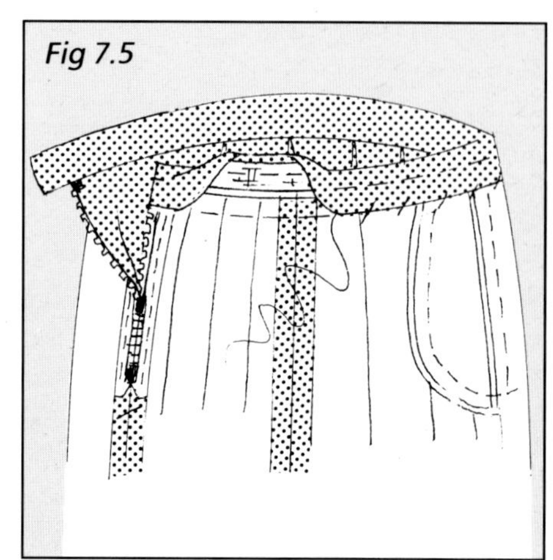

Fig 7.5 Hem the band to the stitching line.

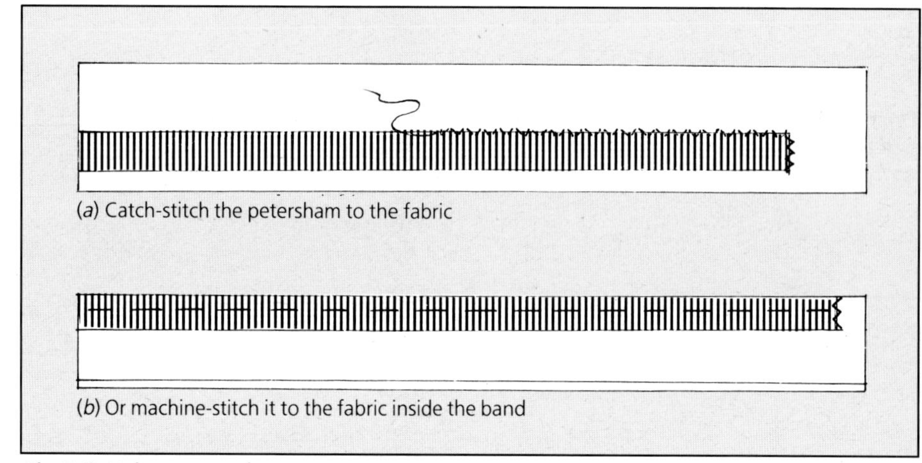

Fig 7.6 Using petersham.

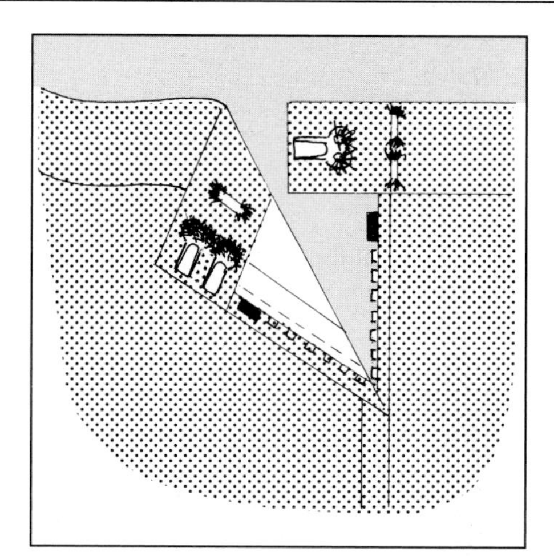

Fig 7.7 Attaching hooks and bars.

WAISTBAND FASTENINGS

Hook and bar fastenings

To finish off the skirt waistband, you can simply use hooks and bars. But you may find that, in several months' time, after carelessly fastening the hooks in too much of a hurry and catching the threads instead of the bars, you will have a frayed end to your waistband. So hooks and bars are not the ideal answer, but they are easy to attach.

Sew two hooks on to the underside of the top band, through one layer of fabric and the interfacing. Sew two bars on the underneath band to correspond. Sew a third *bar* on to the underside of the top band and a *hook* on the underneath band to correspond. Placed this way, the third bar helps to hold the ends more firmly. Use a blanket stitch to attach the hooks and bars (Fig 7.7).

Buttons and buttonholes

On thin fabrics the waistband can be fastened with a button and buttonhole (see pages 78–9).

Fig 7.8 Trouser bar fastening.

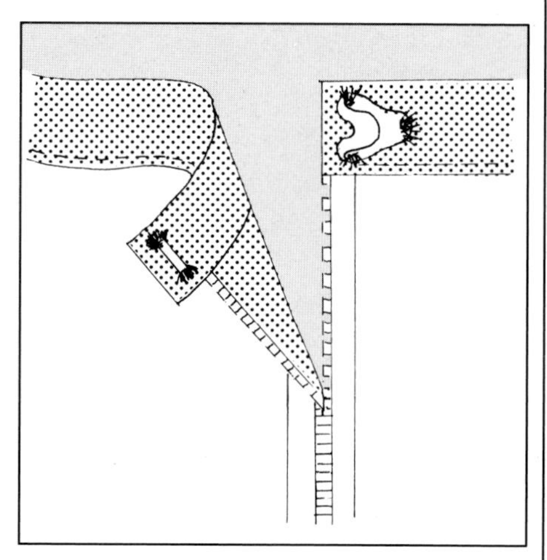

Trouser bar fastenings

The special flat, metal hooks and thin bars which are sold for trouser waistbands are also ideal for skirts in all but lightweight fabrics. Only one hook and one bar are needed for a waistband, and they are stitched in the same way as above (Fig 7.8).

No-sew fasteners

This is the type of fastener used in ready-made skirts. The metal hook and bar have small teeth which are pressed into the fabric before the band is finished, so that they can be hammered and bent over to hold the fabric inside the band. Follow the maker's instructions if you use these.

Once the waistband is fastened and is fitting comfortably and snugly, you are then ready to level the hemline and finish the skirt. But if you want to line it, the lining is added before the waistband.

LINING A SKIRT

A pattern for a skirt lining is not usually included in a paper pattern, yet most women prefer a lined skirt. And with the exception of cotton summer skirts or skirts made in a jersey fabric, most skirts are improved with a lining: they hang better, are easier to wear and keep their shape longer.

Cutting out a skirt lining

Choose a good quality, lightweight lining fabric in a shade which tones with the skirt fabric.

For straight and A-line skirts, use the same skirt pattern to cut out the lining, shortening it by 5 cm (2 in) at the hem. For pleated skirts, fold in the pleats on the paper pattern and cut this same skirt shape minus the pleats. Leave a slit at the centre back or side seam if necessary for ease of walking. For a full or flared skirt, use a separate straight skirt pattern with the same waist measurement as your own pattern to cut out the lining.

Attaching the lining

Stitch the seams and any darts, remembering to leave the opening for the zip in the *right-hand* side seam to correspond with the opening in the *left* side seam of your skirt, as the finished skirt has the wrong sides of fabric and lining together.

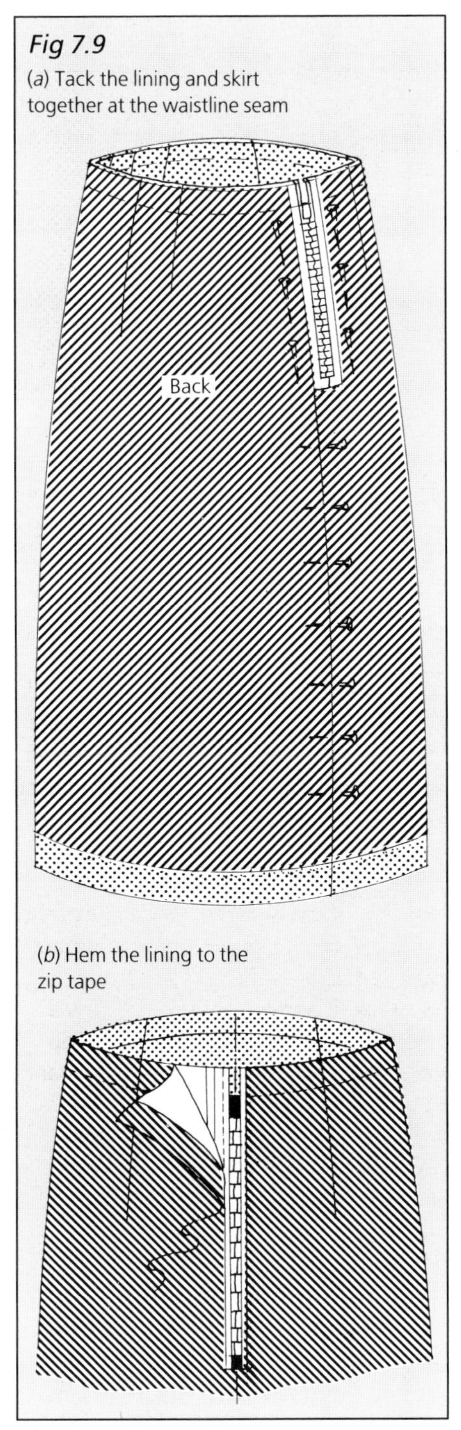

The lining is attached to the skirt with the skirt made up as far as the zip. When the skirt is at this stage, slip the lining, wrong side out, into the skirt, which is right side out, so that the raw edges of the seam turnings are facing. Match the seams, the centre front and back, and tack the waist edges of the lining and skirt together, just above the waist seam line (Fig 7.9*a*). Turn under the seam turnings at the zip, and hem these down on to the zip tape (Fig 7.9*b*). Attach the waistband, stitching through the lining and fabric together.

Finishing the hem of the lining

Turn up the lining hem so that it is about 2.5 cm (1 in) shorter than the skirt hem. The hem can be finished by hand, by using an embroidery stitch on your machine, or by adding narrow lace (Fig 7.10).

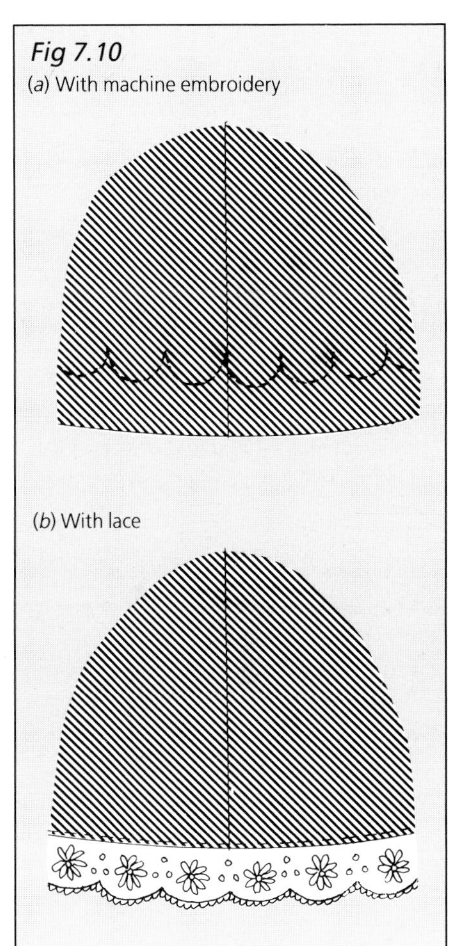

Fig 7.9 Lining a skirt.

Fig 7.10 Finishing the hem of the lining.

LESSON EIGHT

Finishing the hem

The finished hemline is very important. It must be neat and inconspicuous and you will have to give some thought to the length, as it is important to get a length which is flattering to you and gives a balanced look overall.

Try on the skirt with a suitable blouse or top, and shoes with the height of heel that you will normally wear with it, and stand in front of a full-length mirror. There is no such thing as a correct or fashionable hemline, but there *is* a length which is balanced and in proportion for *you* and the design of the skirt you are wearing.

You must find this balanced line by trial and error. Turn up the front of your skirt with pins to the length you feel looks right. (Do not bother about accuracy at this stage.) Then stand a little further back from the mirror and assess the all-over look. Do not hold the skirt in against the front of your legs, but let it hang freely. And if you will want to wear the skirt with a jacket or waistcoat, put that on as well. If you are not happy with this length, then adjust it up or down until you are.

When you have decided on a balanced finished length, leave in one pin to mark it and let the hem down again.

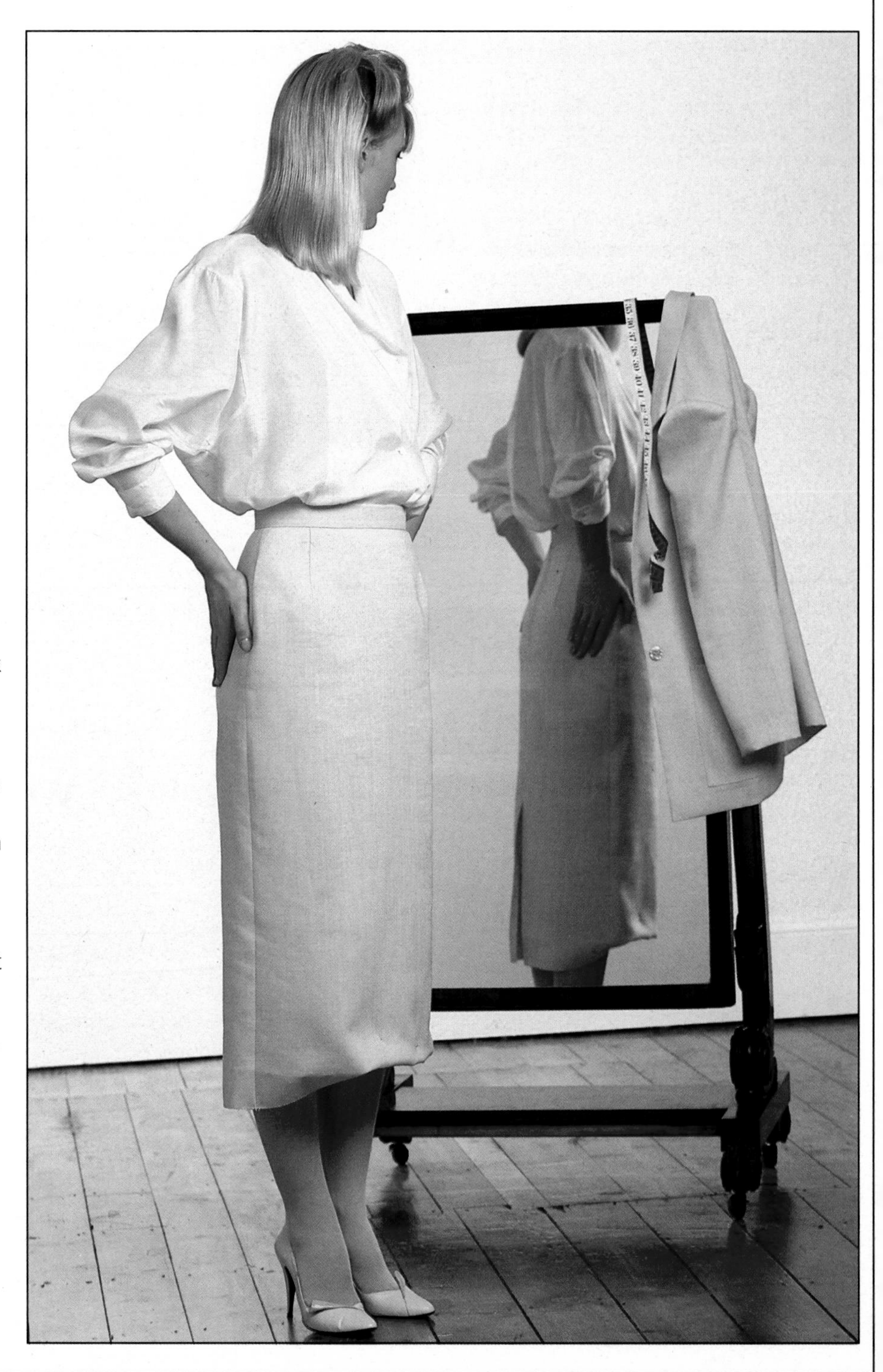

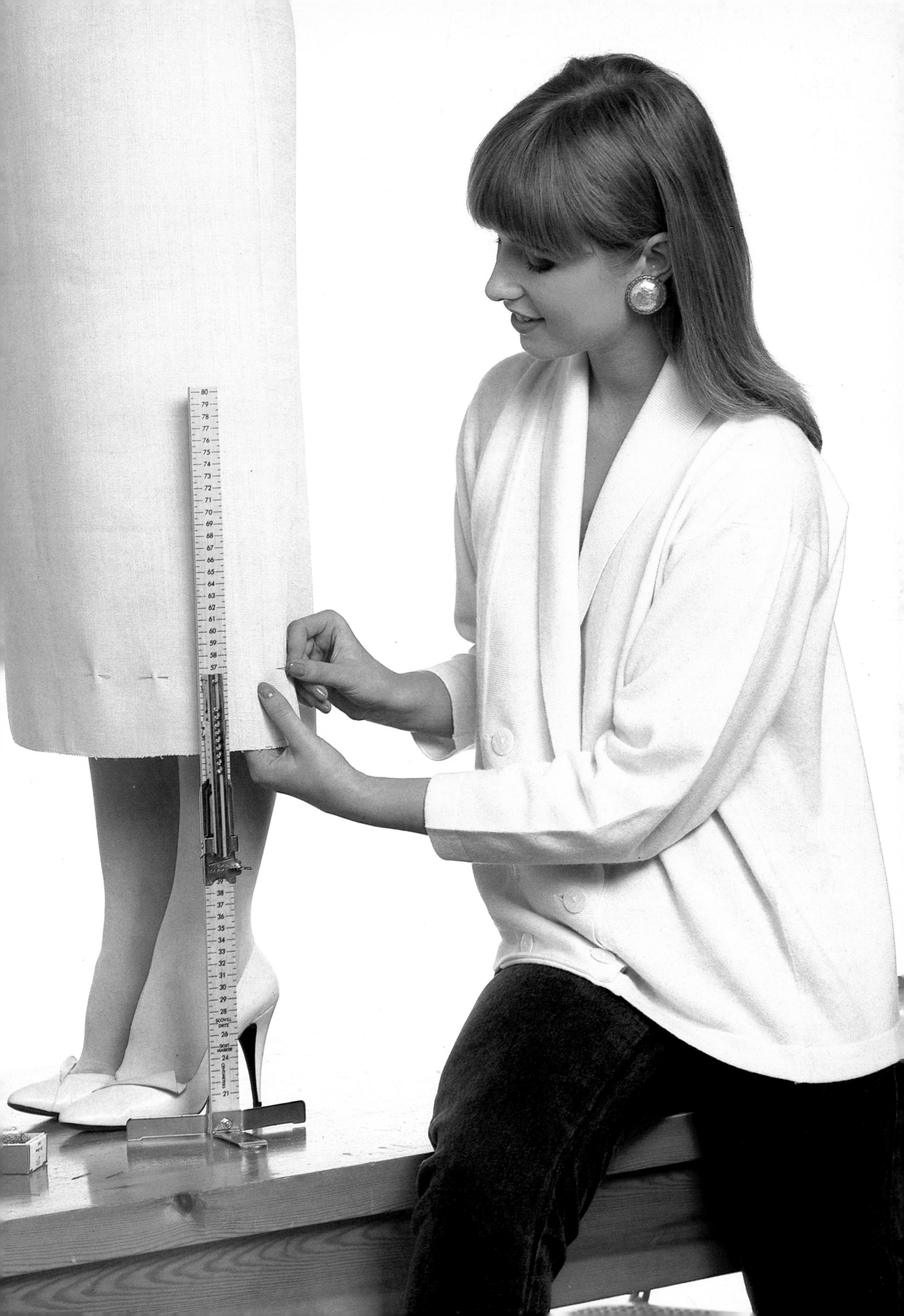
SCOVILL
DRITZ
SKIRT
MARKER
CENTIMETERS

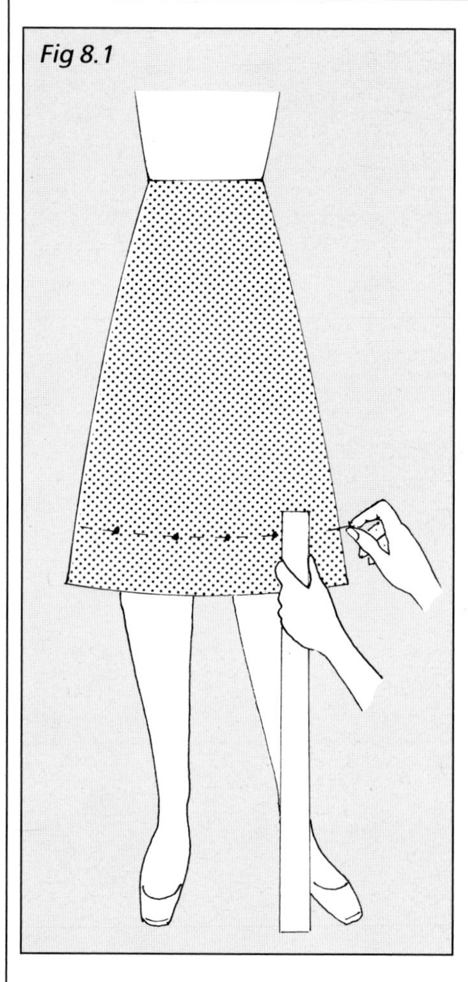

Fig 8.1 While you stand still, your helper moves the hem marker round the hem.

Fig 8.2 You can mark the hem yourself with a chalk puffer.

Fig 8.3 Join up the pins with a line of chalk.

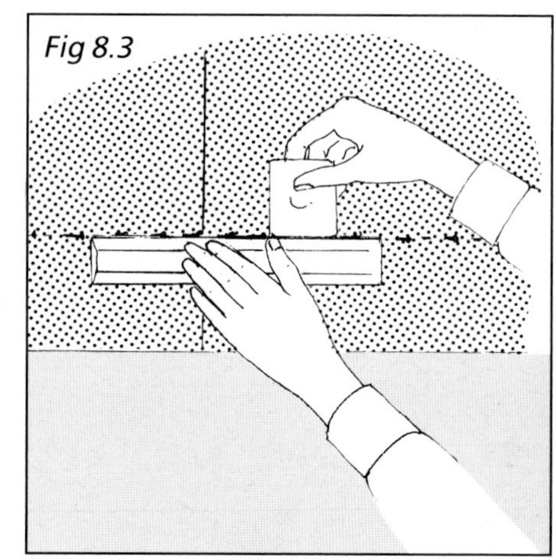

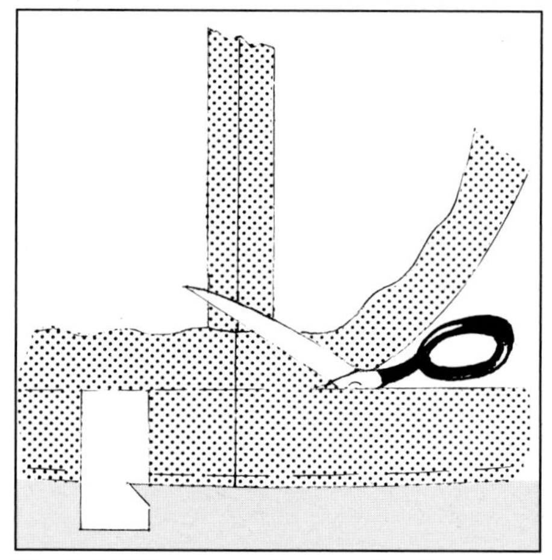

Fig 8.4 Trim away the surplus from the hem.

MEASURING THE HEM

You will need a hem marker or a metre rule for this. A hem marker with a firm tripod base is best as it leaves your hands free.

Get someone to help you to measure up the hem. Stand on a sturdy table and *stand still*. This is important. Get the person who is helping you to adjust the hem marker to the pin which is marking the required hemline. While you stand still, your helper goes round the table, moving the hem marker as she goes, putting in a pin every 10 cm (4 in) or so to mark the line for the hem (Fig 8.1).

This is the ideal way to get an accurate hemline, and also the quickest. It may not always be possible to get someone to help you, but it is possible to buy a hem marker incorporating a stand and a puffer with which you can puff a line of chalk round the hem as you turn (Fig 8.2). As it means that you have to do the moving, it is not as accurate as the above method.

MARKING THE HEM

When you have a satisfactory line of pins marking the required finished length, take the skirt off carefully and lay it flat on a table. Join up the pins with tailor's chalk and a ruler, in an even curve, discarding any pins which are obviously out of line (Fig 8.3).

Turn up the hem on this chalk line and tack along the folded edge. Press this folded edge lightly. (Place the skirt hem lengthways flat, on the ironing board. Do not drape the skirt over the edge of the ironing board as this tends to stretch the hem.) Pin up the surplus hem turning and try on the skirt again to check the length.

If you are happy with it, trim away the surplus hem turning (Fig 8.4). The depth of the hem turning should *never* be more than 5 cm (2 in). On slightly flared or A-line skirts, it should be less – about 3–4 cm (1¼–1½ in) – and on *very* full skirts, trim it away to about 1.5 cm (⅝ in) and finish the hem by machine.

Fig 8.6 To catch-stitch the hem, turn the hem back on itself and work from inside the hem.

Fig 8.7 Using two rows of machine-stitching looks effective.

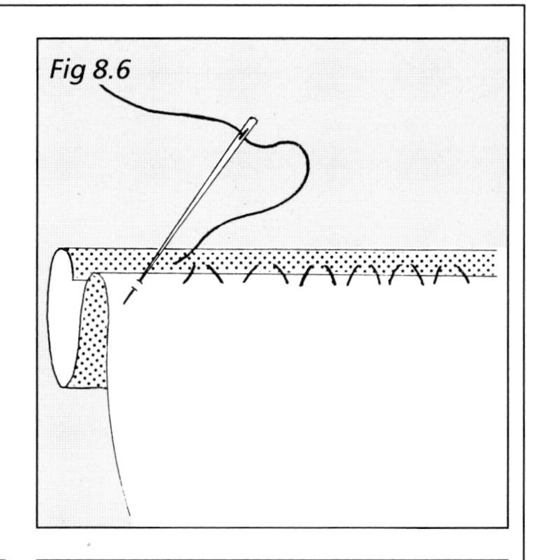

Fig 8.6

NEATENING THE EDGE OF THE HEM

First, neaten the raw edge of the hem. This is usually best done with a zig-zag stitch on your machine (Fig 8.5*a*). If you are using a tweed or medium-weight woollen fabric, the hem is best neatened with a seam binding (Fig 8.5*b*). If you are using a lightweight fabric which frays readily, you will get a neater result by turning under 6 mm (¼ in) at the hem and edge-stitching by machine (Fig 8.5*c*).

After neatening the edge, tack up the hem about 6 mm (¼ in) from the edge.

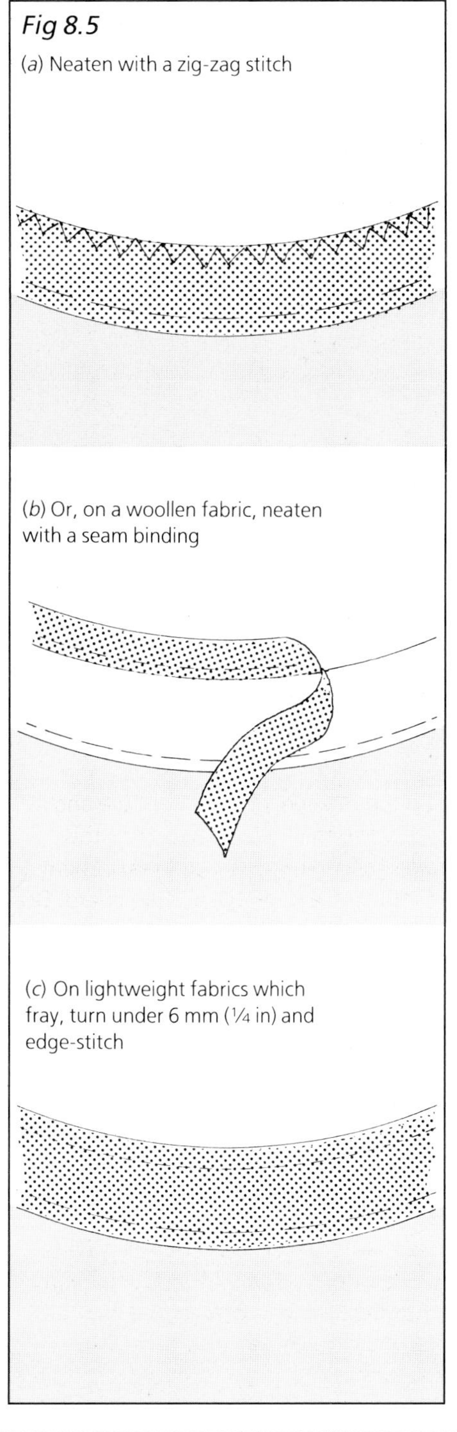

Fig 8.5

(*a*) Neaten with a zig-zag stitch

(*b*) Or, on a woollen fabric, neaten with a seam binding

(*c*) On lightweight fabrics which fray, turn under 6 mm (¼ in) and edge-stitch

Fig 8.5 Neatening the edge of the hem.

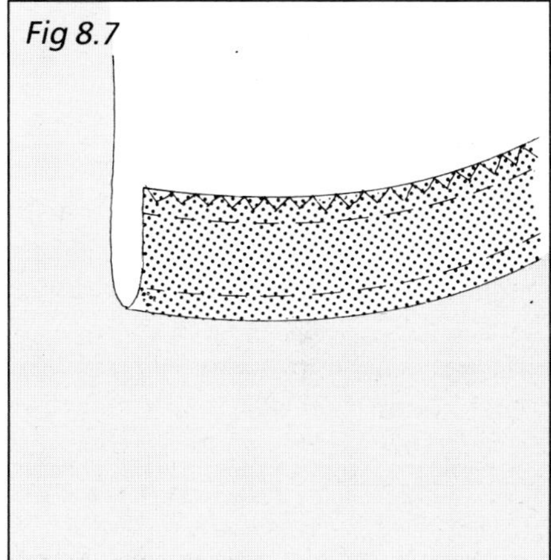

Fig 8.7

STITCHING THE HEM

Catch-stitching the hem

The final stitching of the hem is worked from the inside. Turn the hem back on itself so that the fold is towards you and you are looking inside the hem. Use a very small needle and a matching thread and catch-stitch the fold to the inside of the hem invisibly. Take a small stitch from the hem edge and then a *single thread only* from the garment, then another stitch from the hem edge, and so on (Fig 8.6). Do not pull the thread tight. Working in this way, no stitches are visible on the right side of the garment and the hem will not be seen as an unsightly ridge.

Machine-stitching a hem

A narrow hem on a very full skirt is finished with one or two rows of machine-stitching. Finish the edge with a narrow zig-zag and stitch with a good match of thread and a small stitch, 7 mm (slightly more than ¼ in) in from the fold. A second row of stitching on the fold looks effective (Fig 8.7).

SOME DIFFICULT AREAS IN A HEM

Pleats

Pleats in a seam should have as much surplus fabric as possible trimmed away at the hem to reduce the extra bulk and give a sharp edge to the pleat. Snip across the turnings at the edge of the hem, almost to the stitching line. Press open the turnings below this point and then trim them to 3 mm (⅛ in) (Fig 8.8).

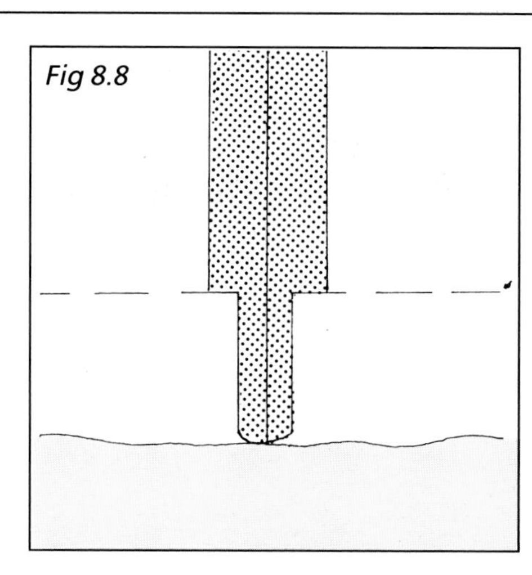

Fig 8.8 Trim the turnings in the hem.

To press the pleat so that it lies in the right direction, snip the seam turning at the edge of the hem, almost to the stitching line (Fig 8.9).

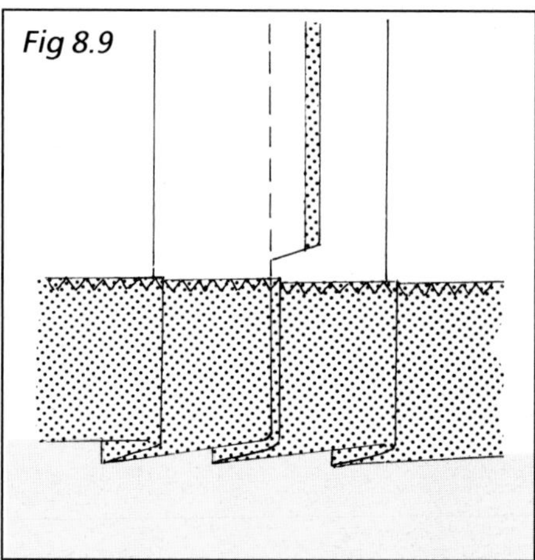

Fig 8.9 Snip the seam turnings at the edge of the hem in a pleat.

Alternatively, you can avoid this problem altogether by finishing the hem *before* you stitch the seam and make the pleats. The finished hem length must be checked very carefully and the hem turned up in the usual way. Then stitch the seams and form the pleats. Trim off the corner of the seam turnings and neaten the edges (Fig 8.10).

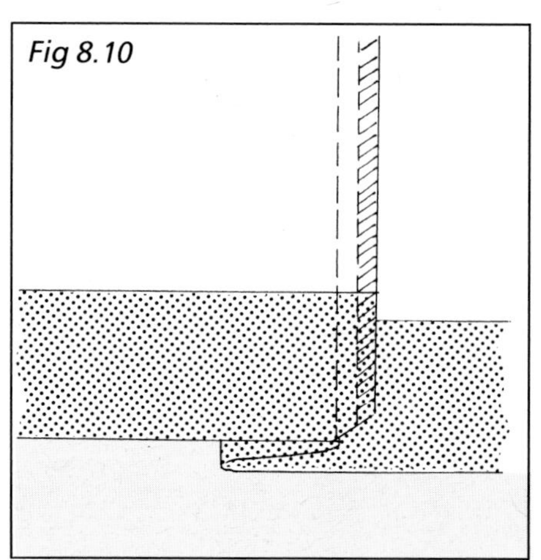

Fig 8.10 An alternative is to finish the hem before forming the pleats.

Fullness in a hem

Surplus fullness in a hem can be minimised by reducing the depth of the hem turning. It should *not* be formed into tiny pleats. In an A-line skirt most of the fullness in the hem is at the side seams. With a woollen fabric this can be shrunk quite easily and disappears in a most satisfying way!

Run a gathering thread each side of the seam at the hem edge (Fig 8.11). Ease up the fullness to fit, keeping the seams on top of one another. Slip a thin card between the hem and the skirt fabric, and hold a steam iron, or a damp cloth over the point of the iron, above the gathered hem edge. When the wool becomes damp, gently nudge the fibres together with the point of the iron so that the material lies flat (Fig 8.12). A pure wool shrinks readily, but with a mixture of wool and other fibres, more steam and more persistence is required.

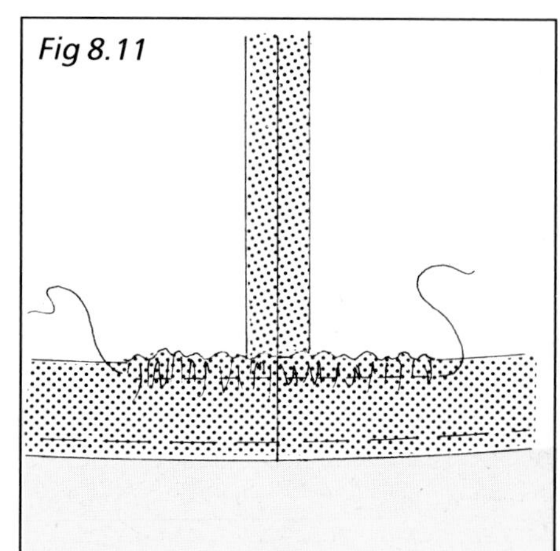

Fig 8.11 Draw up the fullness with a gathering thread.

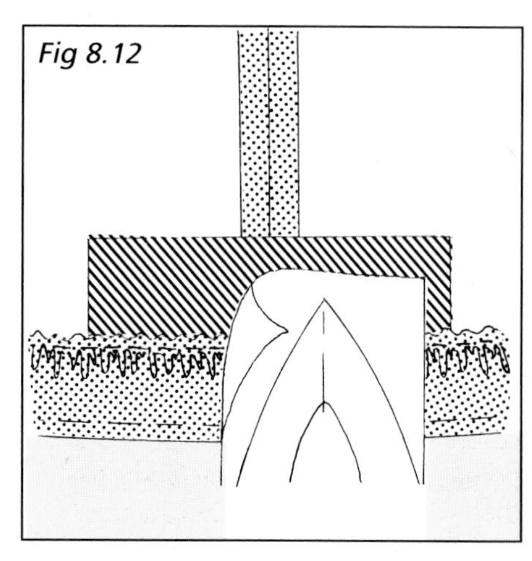

Fig 8.12 Gently nudge the fibres together with the point of the iron.

So, with the first project, the skirt, now successfully completed, you will have mastered several new techniques – a zip, a waistband and a hem. If you are a total beginner, it is a good idea to make a second skirt in a different fabric and using a different pattern so that you gain a little more confidence before you go on to the next simple project, making a sleeveless top.

LESSON NINE

Making a simple top

After your skirt, where the stitching is mostly uncomplicated straight lines, making a simple top to wear with it will introduce you to curved edges, facings and interfacings and a little seam neatening (not to be overdone!).

There are dozens of very attractive, easy tops in the pattern catalogue. At this stage, choose a sleeveless or dolman-sleeved pullover top with a faced or cowl neckline. The faced neckline can be round, square, boat-shaped or V-shaped. This way, you will avoid fastenings and set-in sleeves, which you will meet when you go on to make a shirt-type blouse and a dress.

Choose the pattern for your top by your bust size, referring to your personal measurement chart. Whatever style you choose for your top, the instructions for applying the interfacing and dealing with shaped neck edges will apply.

Choose a fabric for the pattern which will co-ordinate with your skirt. You could, perhaps, even use the same fabric, so that, worn together, with the top tucked in and a wide belt at the waist, the outfit looks like a dress. Alternatively, use a knit fabric for your top, to make a versatile T-shirt top which you can wear with the skirt and team up with the unlined jacket in Lesson Twelve. Read through the chapter on choosing your fabric again to identify any problems in the design, one-way, checks, etc.

Follow the previous instructions for cutting out and thread marking. This should present no problem as there are very few pieces in any pattern for a pull-on top.

Fig 9.1 Stay-stitching.

Fig 9.2 Turn down a single turning at the top of the pocket.

Fig 9.3 Pocket seam turnings.

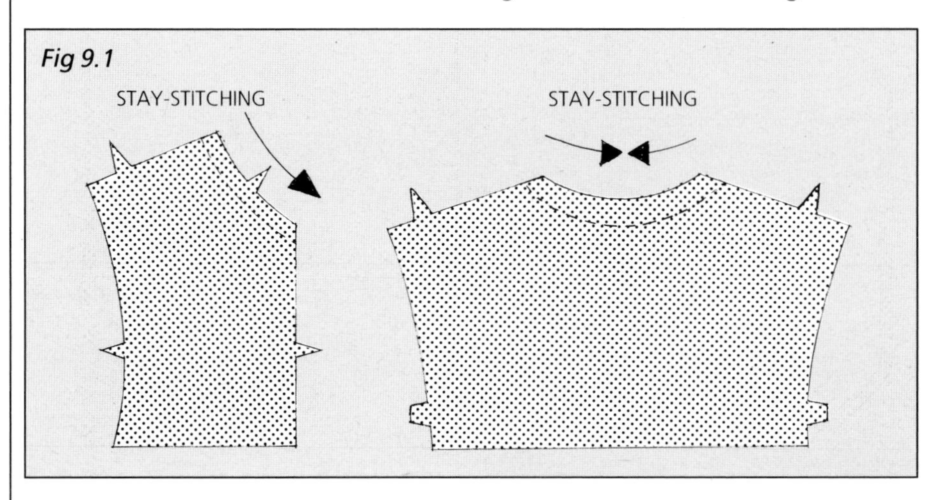

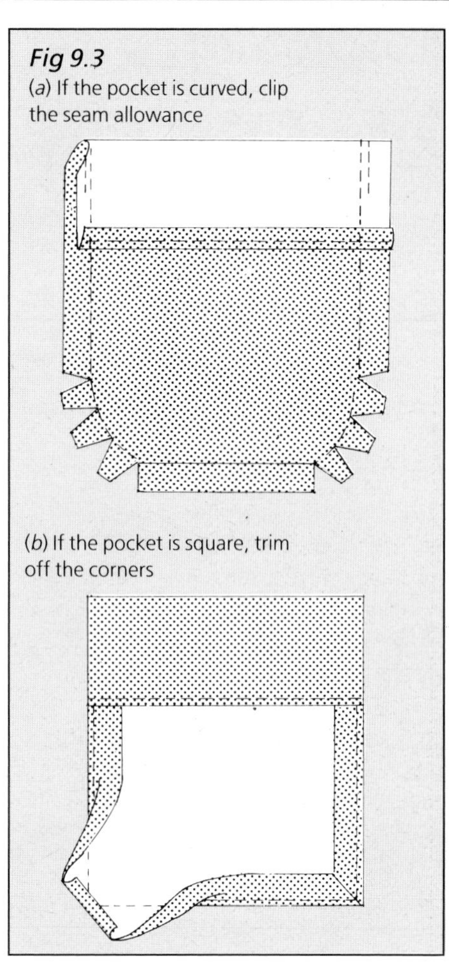

STAY-STITCHING

The first instruction you will be given in the pattern primer is to stay-stitch the curved neck edges. This is done to prevent them stretching as you work.

Stitch, using a long machine stitch or a small hand running stitch, 1.2 cm (½ in) from the cut edge, through the single thickness of fabric and keeping the fabric flat (Fig 9.1).

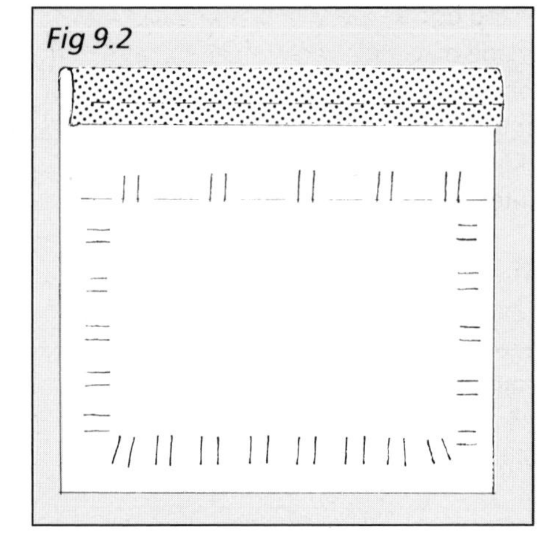

SIMPLE POCKETS

After stay-stitching, the next stage is usually to join the shoulder seams and press them open, unless your pattern includes a small pocket, in which case it is easier to make up the pocket and stitch it at this stage to the front of the blouse with the fabric flat.

The simplest pocket shape is cut from single fabric, has the top neatened with a hem and has turnings to the inside of the pocket.

Mark the position of the pocket on the blouse front and the stitching line of the pocket itself accurately. Turn down a single turning of 6 mm (¼ in) to the wrong side at the top edge of the pocket. Stitch near the fold (Fig 9.2). Fold the top hem on the fold line to the *right* side. Tack and stitch on the seam line at each edge of the hem, continuing the stitching round the pocket, whether curved or straight, on the seam line. This line acts as a guide to keep the pocket shape accurate.

Trim the seam line at the top hem edges to 6 mm (¼ in). If the pocket is curved, clip the seam allowance, removing small wedges, so that the turnings can lie flat when turned to the underside (Fig 9.3*a*). If the pocket is square, trim off the corners (Fig 9.3*b*).

Fig 9.4 Edge-stitch the pocket and reinforce the corners by stitching a small triangle.

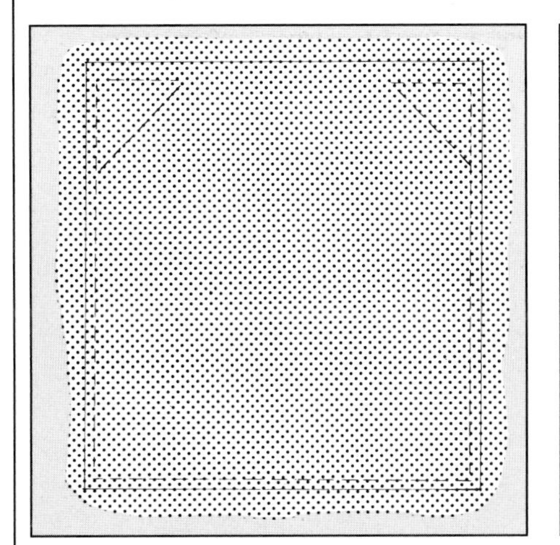

Fig 9.5 Stitch, leaving a break in the stitching.

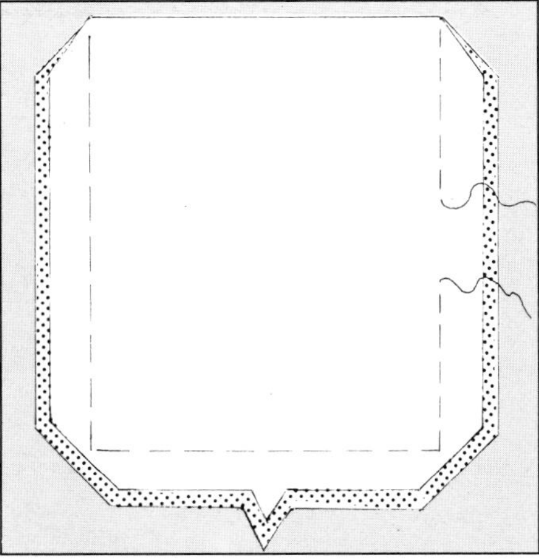

Fig 9.6 Slip-stitch the opening together.

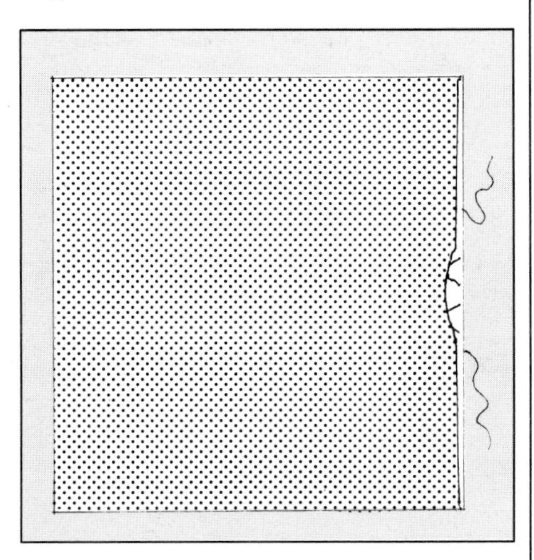

Turn the top hem to the wrong side and press. Tack and press the seam turnings on the other sides of the pocket to the wrong side, turning the line of machine stitching under so that it will not show on the right side.

Tack the pocket in position on the blouse front. Using a small machine stitch, edge-stitch close to the pocket edge, reinforcing the corners by stitching diagonally, to form a small triangle (Fig 9.4). (Several other ways of top-stitching a pocket for a bold effect are given on page 70.)

A top pocket for a shirt blouse can also be made of double fabric, giving a self-lined pocket. This avoids the seam turnings on the inside edges, where fluff collects, and it gives a little extra firmness without interfacing.

The pocket and the self lining are cut in one piece. Fold the pocket in half along the fold line, right sides together. Stitch right round the pocket on the seam allowance line, leaving a break in the stitching (Fig. 9.5).

Trim the seam line to 6 mm (¼ in) and cut off the corners. Turn the pocket right side out through the opening. Ease out the corners gently with a pin. Roll the seam line between the thumb and forefinger so that it lies on the edge, and tack round the pocket on the outside edges, turning in the open edges in the seam. Slip-stitch the opening together (Fig 9.6) and then press. Stitch to the blouse front as above.

Once the pockets are in place, the neck opening is dealt with, before the side seams are joined.

A FACED NECKLINE

A neck opening which is neatened with self fabric is called a faced neckline. A facing is a flat piece of fabric that is cut to the same shape as an edge and is stitched to the right side and turned under to the wrong side to neaten it. Occasionally, you will come across a pattern where the facing has been turned to the outside of the neckline as a decorative feature. Facings are used on neck edges, armhole edges, and front and back openings.

INTERFACING

A facing is reinforced to keep its shape with what is known as *inter*facing. An interfacing is a third layer of fabric which is added to stabilise a curved edge or an opening, or to give extra crispness to collars, cuffs and pocket flaps. It is hidden between the outer garment and the facing. The amount of interfacing required for your pattern is given on the back of the pattern envelope.

The non-woven interfacings on the market, which are made specially for the home dressmaker, are excellent. They are made from fused fibres and have no grain, so they cut economically in any direction. There are two main types, sew-in and iron-on, and it is a matter of personal preference which you choose. The purist chooses sew-in and the dressmaker in a hurry chooses iron-on. Try both at some stage in your sewing and make up your own mind; both give good results.

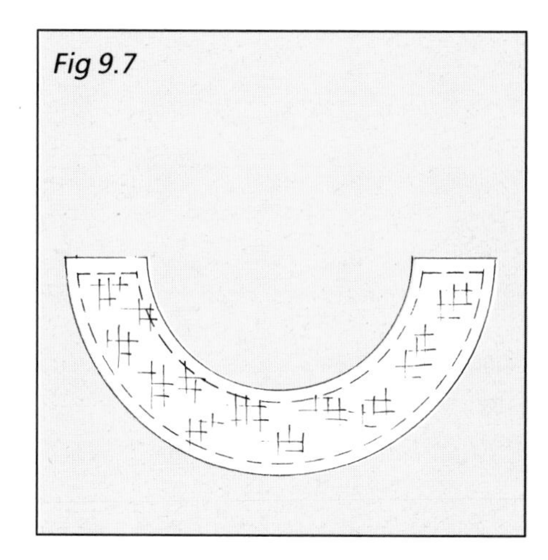

Fig 9.7

The important thing is to get the correct *weight* of interfacing. Each type comes in lightweight or soft, medium and heavy. The interfacing should be just a little lighter than your fabric, never heavier. If you are unsure, try the effect by draping the fabric, backed by the interfacing, over your hand.

A separate pattern is not usually given for the interfacing. Use the *facing* pattern pieces and cut the identical shapes in interfacing.

You can use the interfacing to good advantage if you are a beginner, by drawing your stitching lines in pencil on the interfacing. This way you get the shape of collars and facings exactly right.

First, cut the interfacing, whether sew-in or iron-on, to the size of the facing. Place the interfacing (rough side down if it is iron-on) on the wrong side of the facing. Keep the fabric and interfacing very flat. Tack the facing to the interfacing on the stitching line (Fig 9.7).

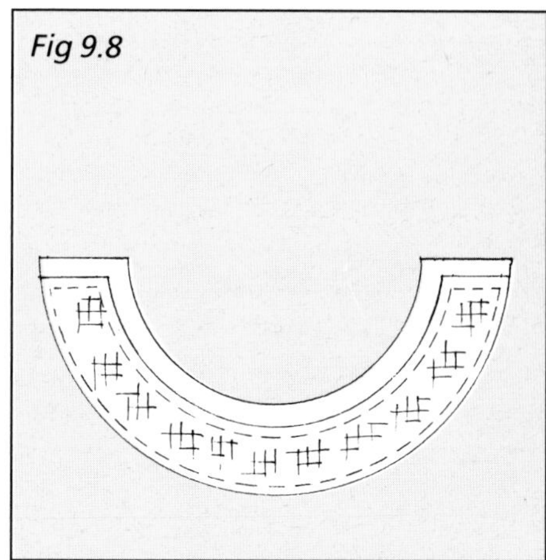

Fig 9.8

Now trim away the seam turnings *of the interfacing only*, just outside the tacking line (Fig 9.8). This is to avoid bulky edges, yet at the same time the interfacing will just be caught into the seam line.

For iron-on interfacing, use a damp cloth and a hot iron to press the interfacing firmly on to the facing. Use an up-and-down movement and firm pressure to get a good bond.

Stitch the facings at the shoulders and press the seams open.

Fig 9.7 Tack the facing to the interfacing on the stitching line.

Fig 9.8 Trim away the seam turning of the *interfacing only*, just outside the tacking line.

SEAM NEATENING

The next stage is to stitch the shoulder seams and press them open. But before you do this, it is a good idea to give some thought to neatening seams at this stage. Personally, I have always found this an unproductive and tiresome chore and my advice would be to do as little of this as you possibly can! If you are making a lined skirt, you can get away with doing none at all, as all the seams are hidden by the lining. But with a top, where the seams are exposed and the garment will be washed frequently, you *will* have to finish the seam edges in some way to prevent them fraying. That is, unless your fabric does not fray readily, in which case don't bother. You are the only person likely to notice that you haven't finished off all the inside seam edges.

If you do have to neaten the seam edges, do it the easiest way: stitch round them all, with the fabric flat, *before* you join up the seams. Use a small, neat zig-zag stitch on your machine. If your machine has a foot to help you guide the edge of the fabric to keep it straight, use it and you will be able to stitch fairly rapidly along the edges of the fabric (Fig 9.9).

If you are making up a knit fabric, or a loosely fitting style, use the stitch on your sewing machine which neatens and stitches in one operation. This is a combination of a stretch stitch and a zig-zag stitch (Fig 9.10). With this stitch the seams are not pressed open, but the edges are sealed together.

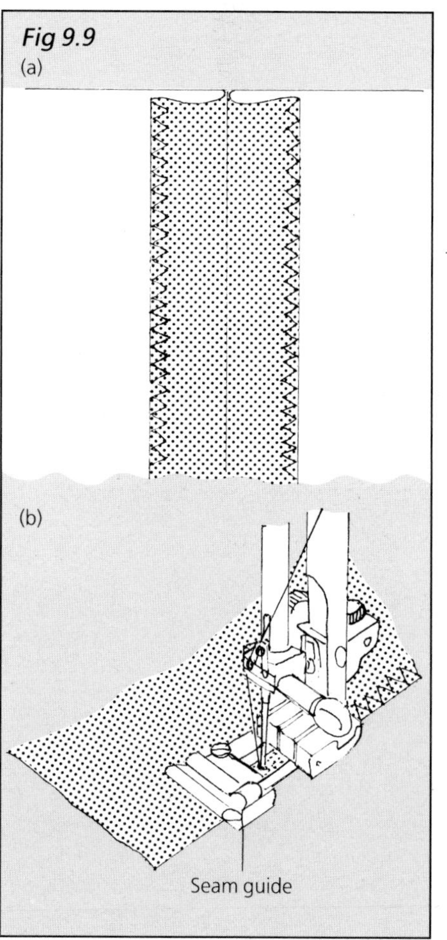

Fig 9.9 Neatening seams using a small, neat zig-zag stitch.

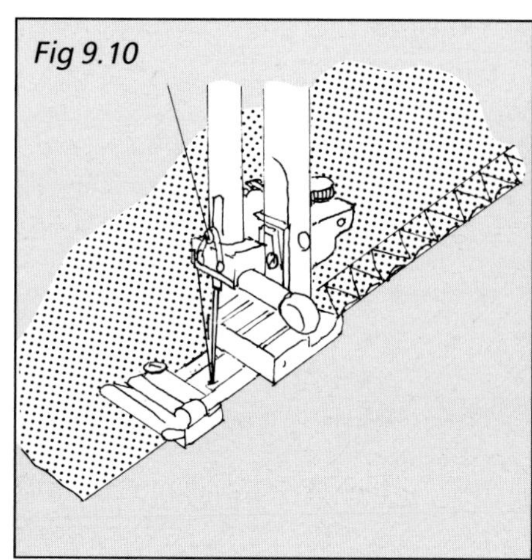

Fig 9.10 Neatening and stitching in one operation.

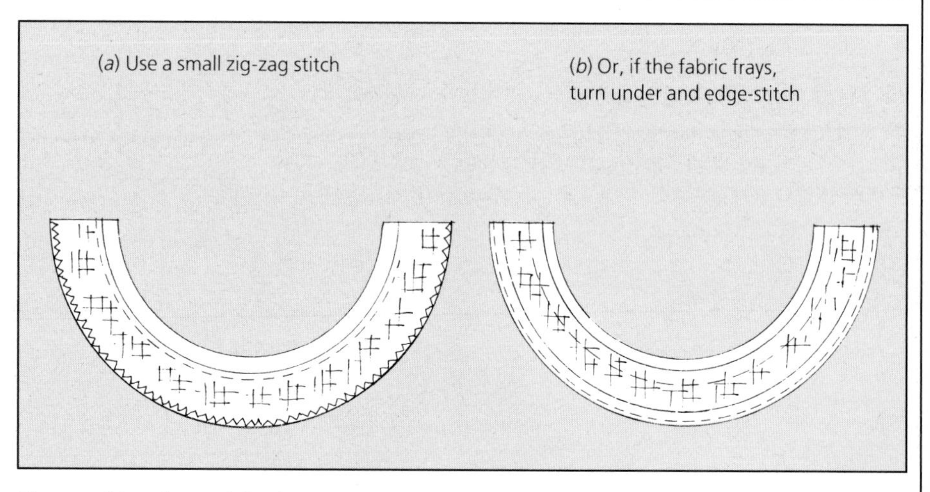

Fig 9.11 Neatening the outer edge of the facing.

The outside edges of the facing must also be neatened. The best way to do this is work a neat zig-zag machine stitch round the outside edge (Fig 9.11*a*). This keeps the edge flat and inconspicuous. If the fabric frays badly, turn under 6 mm (¼ in) and edge-stitch (Fig 9.11*b*).

ATTACHING FACINGS

Work with the garment right side out and place the facing over the neck edge, with right sides together. Match the notches, centre lines and shoulder seams. Tack and stitch along the marked line.

Trimming the seam

This is a very important procedure and one which beginners do not like at all. But you must take courage and trim the neckline seam right down to between 4 and 5 mm (less than ¼ in). Then clip any curves almost to the stitching line every 1.5 cm (⅝ in) (Fig 9.12). With a square neckline, clip right into the corners (Fig 9.13). With a V-shaped neckline, clip almost to the stitching line at the point of the 'V' (Fig 9.14). Turn the facing to the inside of the garment.

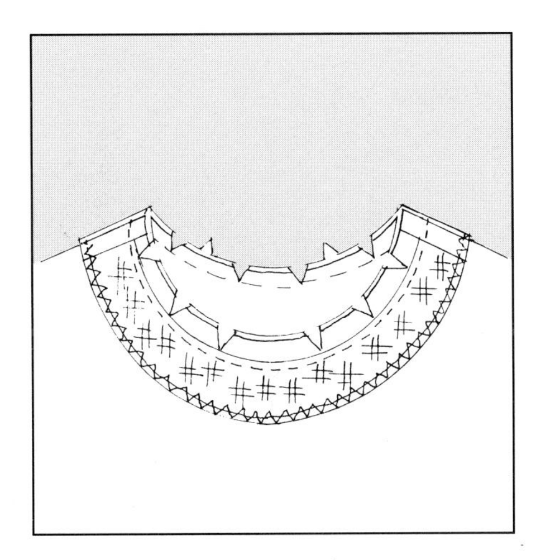

Fig 9.12 Clip the curves almost to the stitching line.

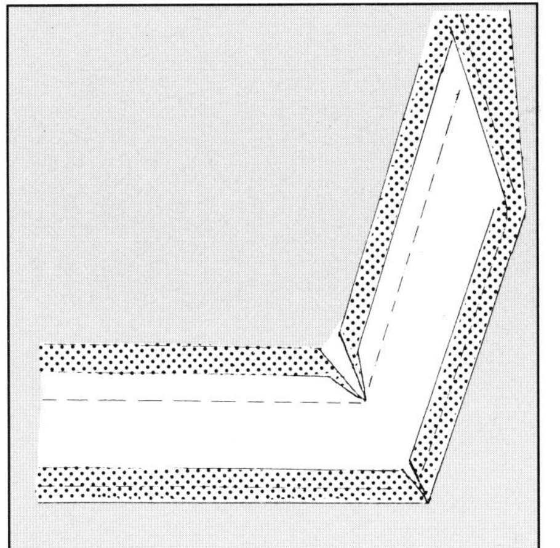

Fig 9.13 Clip into the corner of a square neckline.

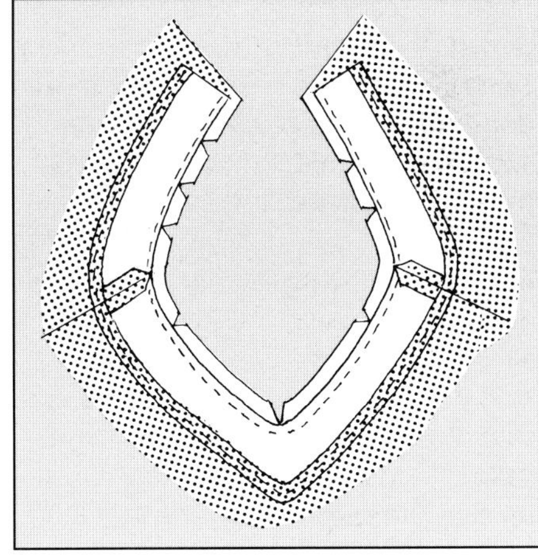

Fig 9.14 Clip to the point of the 'V'.

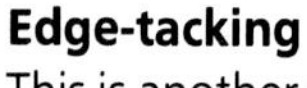

Edge-tacking

This is another very important technique and if you omit this stage on any edges – facings, collars or fronts – you will never achieve a professional look to your clothes.

Work the seam between your finger and thumb, so that it is at the very edge. Tack right on the edge using a small stitch to hold it firmly in place (Fig 9.15). Press the edge, taking care not to stretch it.

The facing is stitched by hand to the garment *at the seams only*.

Understitching

When you have made several tops or dresses with faced necklines, there is a refinement on this procedure you can include, called understitching. Understitching is stitching the facing to the seam turnings, to prevent the edge of the facing from rolling to the right side.

After pressing the facing, remove the edge-tacking. Open out the facing and the seam turnings away from the garment. Machine-stitch through the facing and the turnings only, 3 mm (⅛ in) from the neckline seam (Fig 9.16).

Fig 9.15 Tack right on the edge using a small stitch to hold it in place.

Fig 9.16 Machine through the facing and turnings only.

Fig 9.17 Stitch the collar, matching notches, centres and shoulder seams.

Fig 9.18 Hem the collar down on to the stitching line.

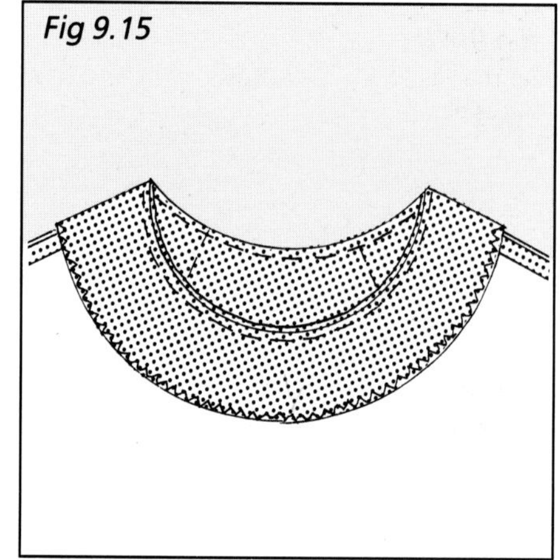

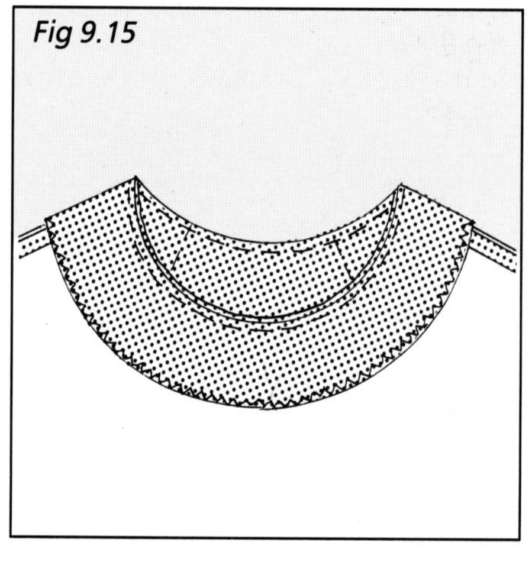

Fig 9.15

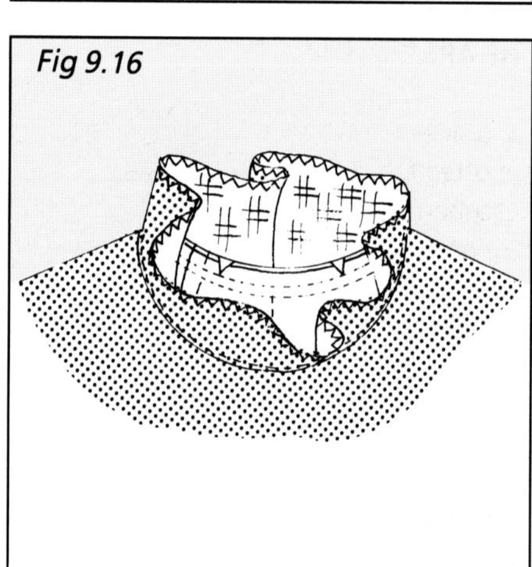

Fig 9.16

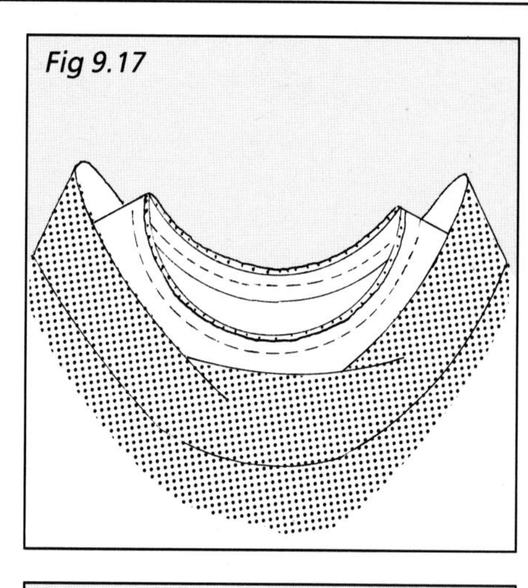

Fig 9.17

Fig 9.18

A COWL OR ROLLED COLLAR NECKLINE

This is a soft neckline which needs no interfacing and very little pressing and is a good choice for a beginner as an alternative to the easy, faced neckline.

Make sure that you cut the collar *exactly* as the pattern suggests to get the correct bias. Stitch the centre back collar seam and press it open.

Work with the garment right side out and place the raw edge of the collar, right sides together, to the right side of the garment, matching notches, centres and shoulder seams. Tack and stitch (Fig 9.17).

Trim and clip the seam exactly as described above. Turn under the seam allowance on the other collar edge and bring this edge down on to the neckline seam. Tack and hand-hem in place (Fig 9.18).

Fig 9.19 Press horizontal darts downwards and vertical darts towards the centre.

Fig 9.20 The blouse hem.

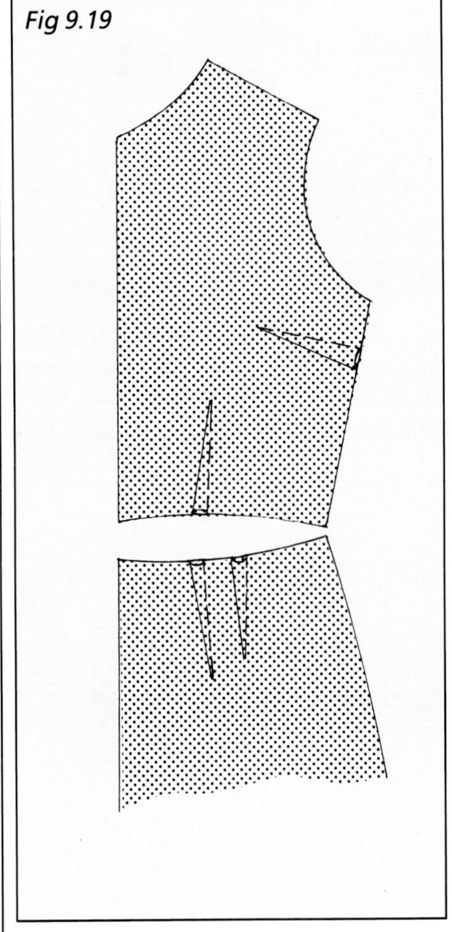

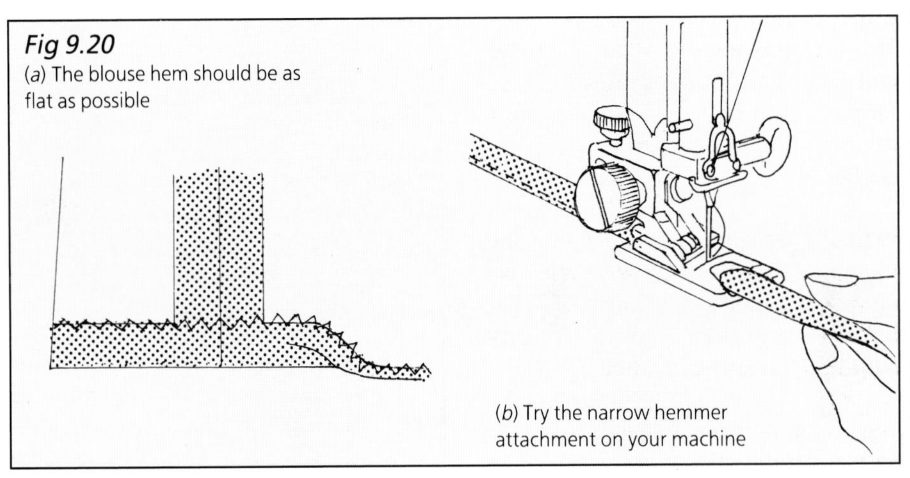

Once the neckline has been stitched, the side seams can be joined and neatened. If there is a dart in the side seam, stitch this in exactly the same way as the skirt dart in Lesson Six. These side seam darts are pressed downwards. Any darts at the waistline are pressed towards the centre (Fig 9.19).

THE ARMHOLE EDGES

For a sleeveless top, the armhole edges are often faced in the same way as described for the faced neckline. Armhole facings are *not* interfaced. It is usually easier to apply the facings before joining the side seams.

With a very simple top, the armhole edges are often finished with a narrow hem. Keep this hem as narrow as possible and stitch it before the underarm seam is stitched or it becomes difficult to turn at the underarm. It can be worked by hand or machine.

THE HEM

The blouse hem should be as flat as possible so that it will not show as a ridge through a slim skirt or trousers. The best way is to make a single, narrow turning, neatened with a zig-zag. This can be stitched by hand or machine (Fig 9.20). When you become expert with your sewing machine, try the narrow hemmer attachment, as this is a neat and speedy alternative way to stitch the hem.

Having mastered a skirt and a simple top, you can now combine the techniques you have learned and go on to make a dress.

LESSON TEN

Making a dress

You can now make a simple dress! It is obvious that the simple top and the skirt in the previous lessons will combine happily into a dress. Many more patterns from the STYLE catalogue are now well within your reach.

I suggest that you stick fairly closely to the same type of faced neckline as in the previous chapter, or that you choose an easy collar, such as a Peter Pan, mandarin or grandfather collar. In other words, avoid the more difficult shirt collar and revers at this stage. (These are included in Lesson Eleven, 'Making a shirt blouse'.)

And as this will be your first attempt at setting in a sleeve, make things easy for yourself and choose a dress with the easiest type of set-in sleeve, one with a gathered top, as this avoids the problem of getting a smoothly rounded sleeve head. (But if you prefer the smooth sleeve head and you do want to jump ahead and try setting in a perfectly smooth sleeve, you can find help with that, when you get to that stage, on pages 88–90.)

So have a look at the dress pattern section. There are some very attractive styles: dropped waistlines, or all-in-one skirt and top, batwing sleeves cut in one with the bodice, pleated and tucked bodices, and full and gathered or slim and straight skirts.

There is a wide choice of fastenings on dress patterns: some pull-over styles have no fastening; other dresses have rouleau ties, zips or buttons. You can avoid buttonholes at this stage, but if there is a pattern you really like and it has buttonholes, refer to page 78 when you get to that stage. The long zip at the back of a dress is put in the same way as the skirt zip in Lesson Five. Refer to Lesson Eight when you come to the hem of the dress.

Re-read the chapter on choosing your pattern, and choose a style you *really* like and which you will *really* enjoy making up.

The new processes which you need to learn now are joining a top to a skirt at the waist (which will involve basic fitting), elasticated waists, a simple Peter Pan collar, or a mandarin or grandfather collar with a faced neck opening, setting in a gathered sleeve, and making rouleau loops and ties.

It is always easier to complete as much as you can of the bodice of a dress before joining it to the skirt. Not only is it easier to handle, but the finished sleeves and neckline could affect the fit when you try on the dress to judge the correct position for the waistline seam. But if you have chosen a pattern with a back zip, it will make a neater finish for the collar or facings at the back neck if you reverse the order and join the bodice and skirt, then put in the zip and finally complete the neck opening.

The neckline should always be finished before inserting a set-in sleeve, as it can affect the balance of the armhole.

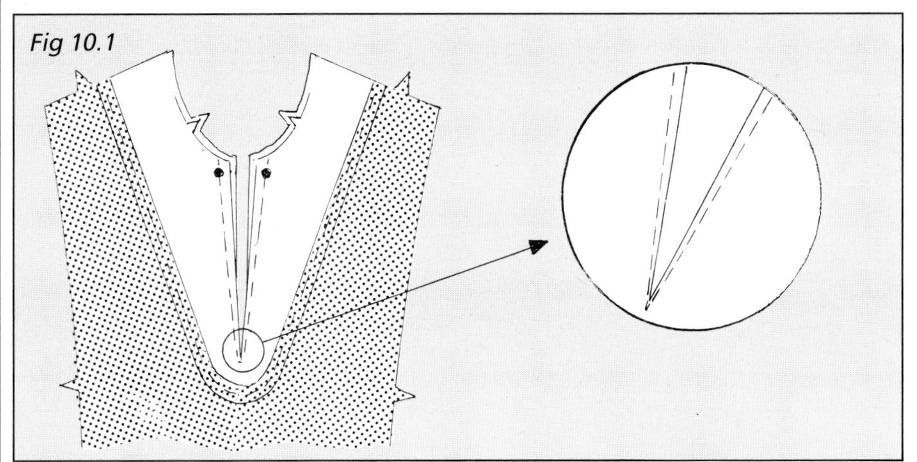

Fig 10.1 Cut the slit right to the stitching line.

Fig 10.2 When turned to the inside, the facing should press flat.

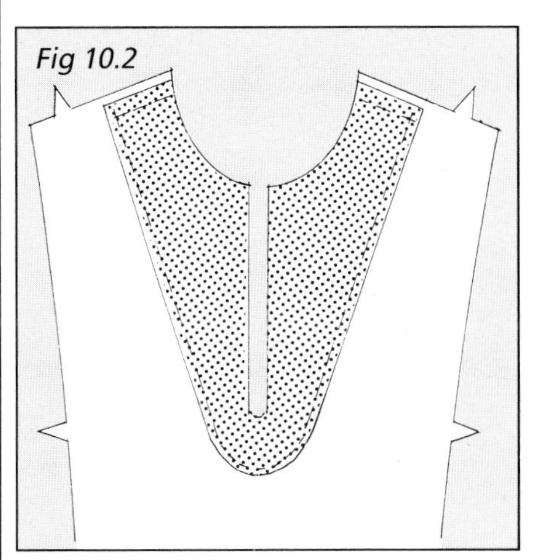

A FACED OPENING

A dress with a faced neckline often has a front slit opening neatened with a facing, and a mandarin collar is often combined with a faced opening. This is applied in exactly the same way as the facing in Lesson Nine, except that the front facing is shaped to include the length of the slit opening.

The important thing here is to make sure that you cut the end of the slit for the opening *right to the stitching line*, without cutting the stitches (Fig 10.1), otherwise, when the facing is turned to the inside, the end of the opening will be puckered and will not press flat (Fig 10.2).

Join the bodice at the shoulders and press the seams open.

TYPES OF COLLAR

The easiest type of collar is a *flat* collar, such as a Peter Pan collar. The neck edge of this type of collar is curved, but there is no roll-over against the neck as the collar lies flat against the bodice (Fig 10.3). The outside edge of this collar and the collar ends can be rounded, scallop-shaped or pointed. It is still a Peter Pan collar if it lies flat against the garment.

The next easiest is the *stand* collar, such as a mandarin collar, or a narrower version of it called a grandfather collar (Fig 10.4). This collar stands upright against the neck, Chinese-style.

The other type of collar is a *roll* collar. This is an almost straight collar attached to a curved neck edge, so that it stands in against the neck and also turns over to frame the face (Fig 10.5*a*). Shirt-type collars are in fact a combination of the roll collar and lapels (Fig 10.5*b*). Although the term 'shirt collar' is used generally for this type of collar, the true shirt collar is mounted on a collar band like a man's shirt, to give a tailored appearance (Fig 10.6). For a shirt-type collar and a shirt collar with a collar band, see pages 71–2.

All collars need to be interfaced to stiffen them. The weight of interfacing depends on the weight of the fabric you are using and the amount of crispness you prefer.

Fig 10.3 Flat or Peter Pan collars.

Fig 10.4 Stand collars.

Fig 10.5 Roll collars. Shirt-type collars are roll collars with lapels.

Fig 10.6 Shirt collar with collar band.

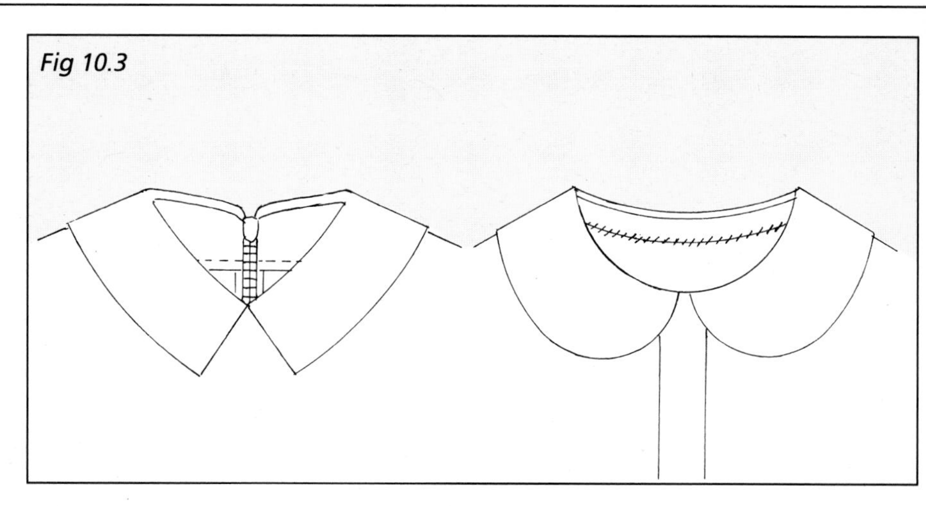

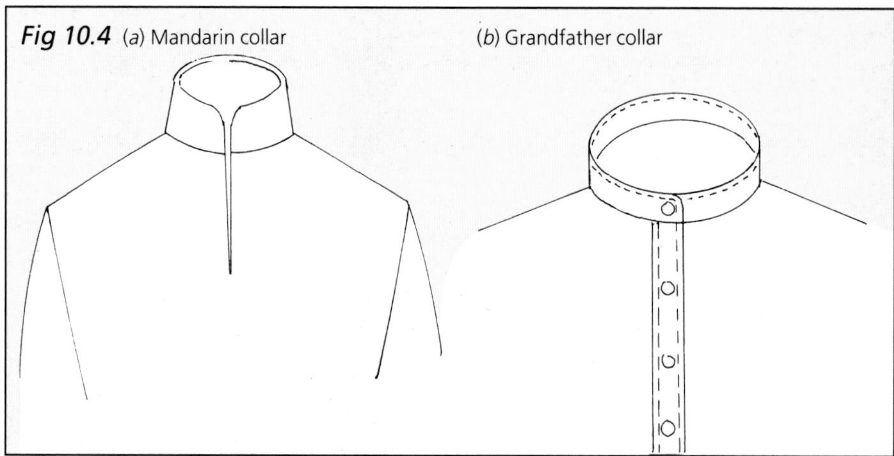

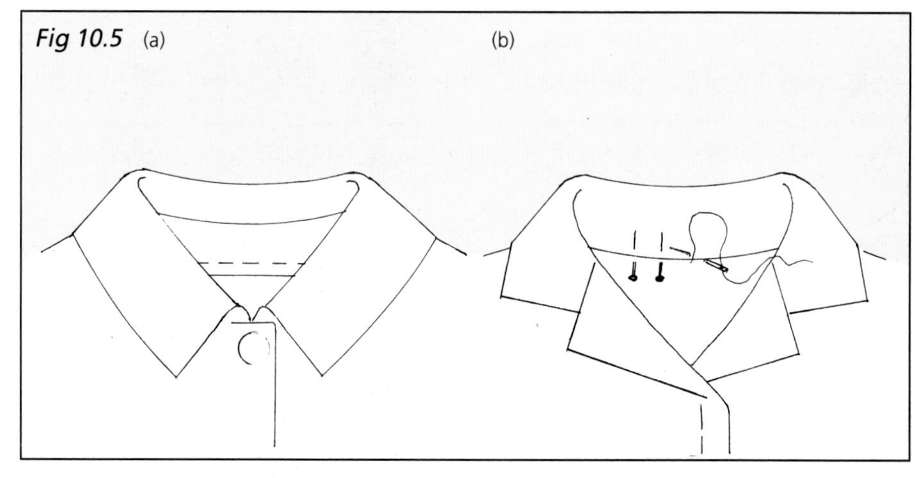

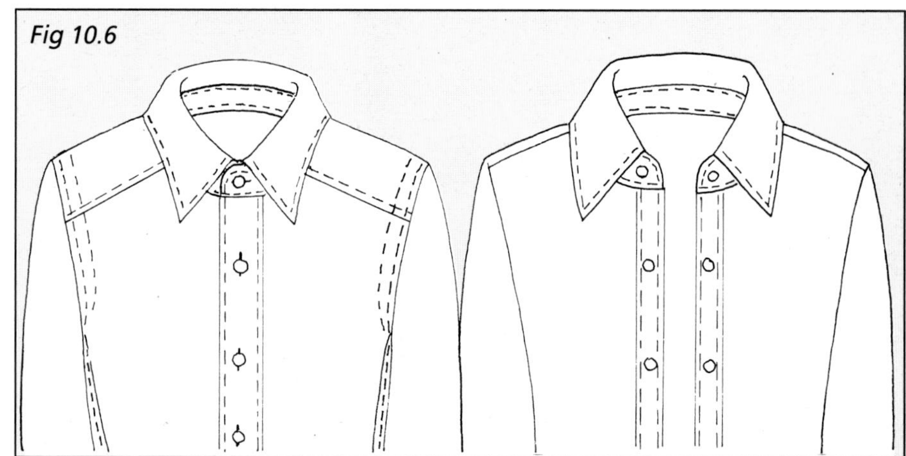

Fig 10.7 Cut out small notches at the curves.

Fig 10.8 Edge-tack the collar.

Fig 10.9 Tack along the marked neckline.

Fig 10.10 Tack and stitch the neckline seam through all thicknesses.

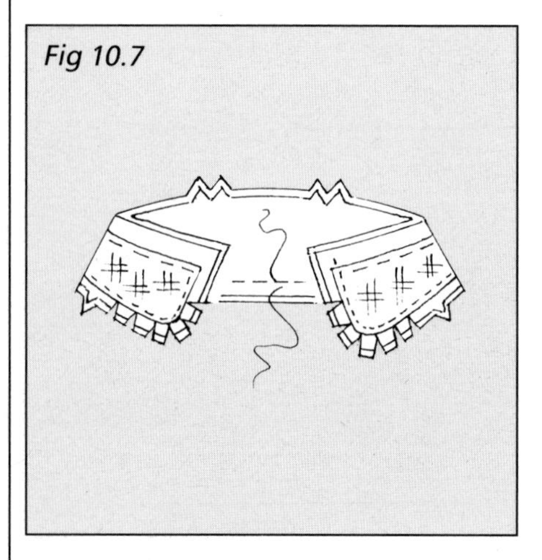

Flat or Peter Pan collars

You may sometimes come across a flat collar attached to the neck edge with a bias-cut binding only. This is usual with nightwear and children's clothes. More often, it is attached with a facing, which is neater and means that the neck can then be worn open or fastened.

To make up a flat collar

Cut the exact collar shape in interfacing and apply the interfacing to one side of the collar, following the instructions in Lesson Nine (cutting away the surplus interfacing in the seam line and pencilling the stitching line on to the interfacing, as a guide for your stitching).

Pin and tack the collar pieces, right sides together, and machine-stitch the marked seam line accurately. Remove the tacking and trim one seam turning to 6 mm (¼ in) and the other to 3 mm (⅛ in). Snip the curved ends, cutting small notches every 1.5 cm (⅝ in) to avoid a lumpy edge to the collar when it is turned (Fig 10.7).

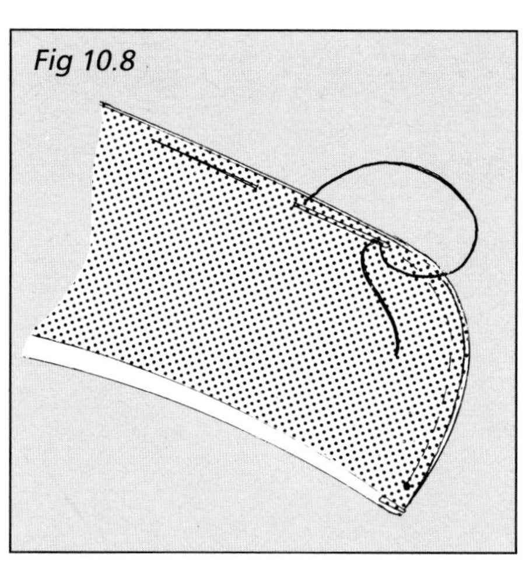

Turn the collar right side out. Work the seam between the finger and thumb so that it lies on the edge, and edge-tack (Fig 10.8). Press well, using a damp cloth and hot iron. Do not remove the edge-tacking yet.

Attaching a flat collar with a complete neck facing

A complete neck facing consists of a shaped back facing as well as a front facing. The front facing is often formed by turning back the fabric on a marked fold line, or by extending the facing used for the front slit opening. The back neck facing is a separate, small pattern piece.

Complete the front facing, following the pattern instructions, and join the front and back facing at the shoulder seams. Press open, and neaten the outside edge of the facing with a small, neat zig-zag stitch, or narrow hem.

Work with the garment right side out and place the collar to the neck edge. Match the centres, notches and shoulder marks. Pin, using the pins vertically. Tack along the marked neckline seam (Fig 10.9).

Place the facing over the collar, matching all the marks and notches. Tack and stitch the neckline seam, through all thicknesses (Fig 10.10).

Trim the seam turnings to 6 mm (¼ in). Turn the facing to the inside (Fig 10.11). Press the inside of the neck edge, using a tailor's ham to press the curve.

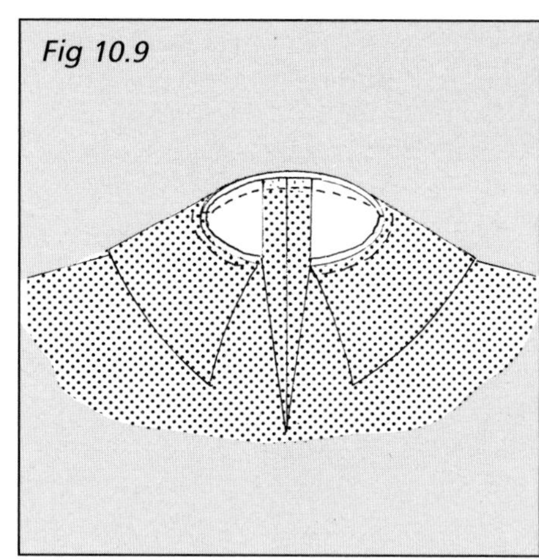

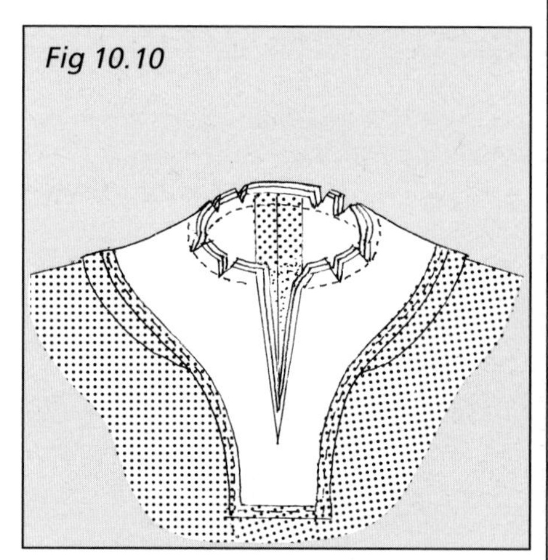

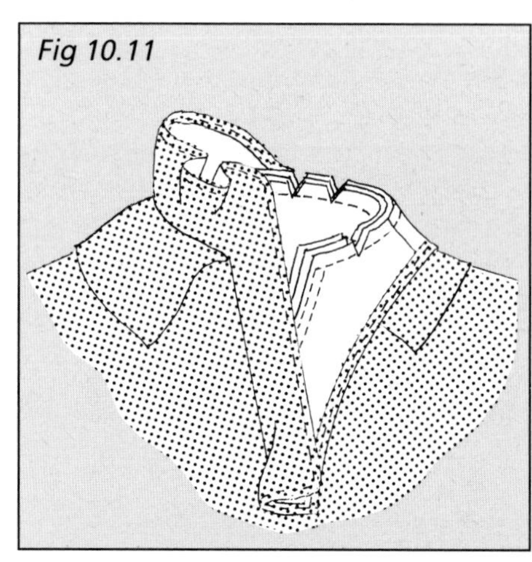

Fig 10.11 Turn the facing to the inside.

Stand collars

Attaching a stand collar with a facing

The mandarin-type stand collar is put on in the same way as the Peter Pan collar when there are front and back facings.

Attaching a stand collar without a facing

Often, however, this type of collar is used to neaten the neck edge alone without the addition of any facing.

Interface one collar piece. Turn under the neck edge seam allowance on the other collar piece and press (Fig 10.12).

Place the two collars with their right sides together, matching the marks and notches. Tack and stitch the outer curved collar edge, along the pencilled stitching line (Fig 10.13). Trim the seams, turn and edge-tack the collar as for the Peter Pan collar. Press well and remove the edge-tacking (Fig 10.14).

Clip the curve of the neck edge almost to the stay-stitching line. Lay the garment flat on the table and straighten out the neck curve (Fig 10.15). Place the interfaced side of the collar to the neck edge. Pin at each end, at the shoulder marks and notches, placing the pins vertically. Ease the two curves to fit, keeping the seam allowance lines together. Tack and stitch along the marked line, taking care not to catch in the free edge of the collar (Fig 10.16). Trim the seam to 6 mm (¼ in). Bring the fold of the other collar down on to the stitching line and hand-hem in place (Fig 10.17).

Attaching a stand collar with a front facing only

Sometimes a collar is put on by a combination of these two methods. The centre front is neatened with a facing, which extends towards the shoulder seam, but there is no separate back facing. The back neck of the collar therefore has to be neatened by turning under the seam allowance and hemming it in place by hand. At the point where the facing ends, the seam allowance is snipped to allow it to turn under. This can be tricky and for a detailed and careful way of doing this, refer to page 71.

Fig 10.12

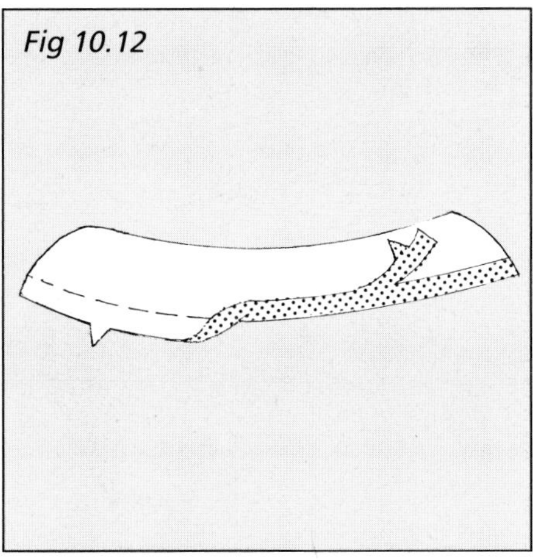

Fig 10.12 Turn under the neck edge seam allowance and press.

Fig 10.13

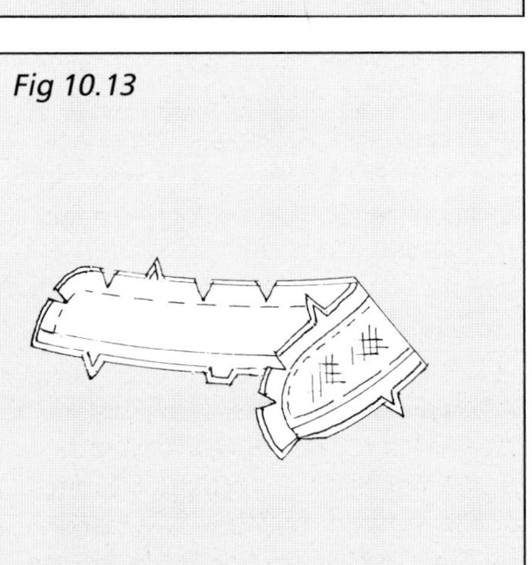

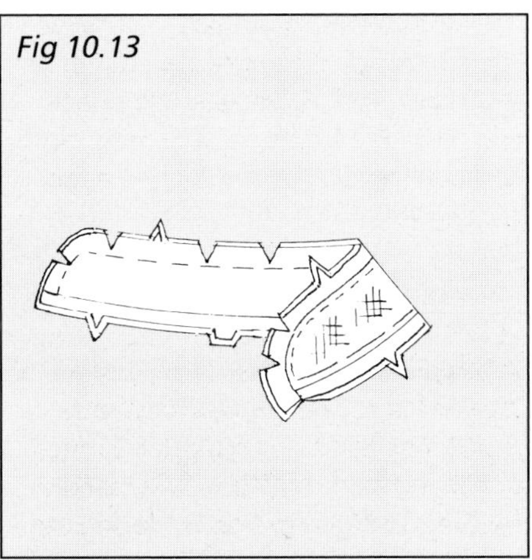

Fig 10.13 Tack and stitch the outer curved collar edge.

Fig 10.14

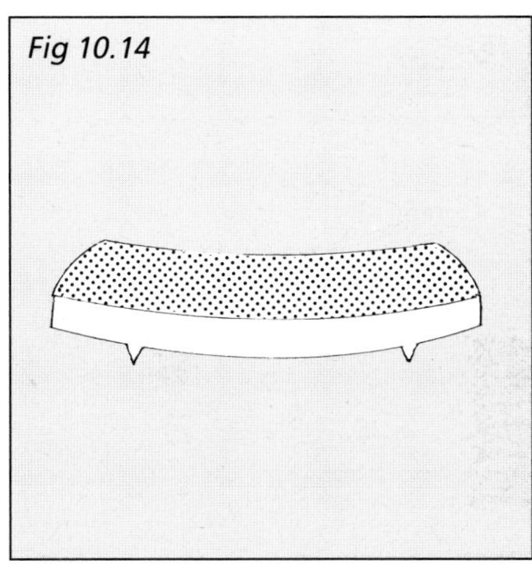

Fig 10.14 Press well and remove the edge-tacking.

Fig 10.15

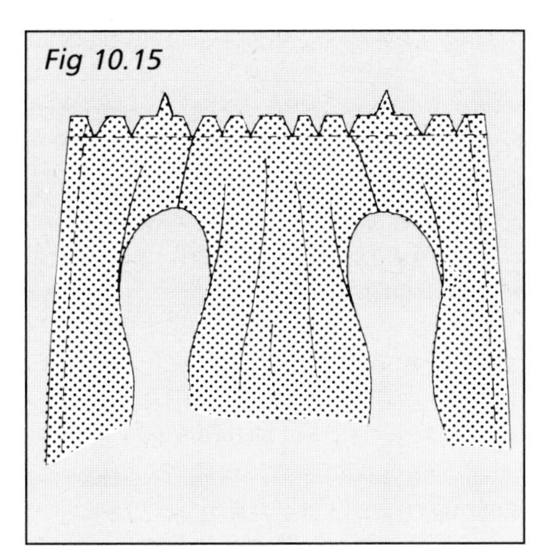

Fig 10.15 Straighten out the neck curve.

Fig 10.16

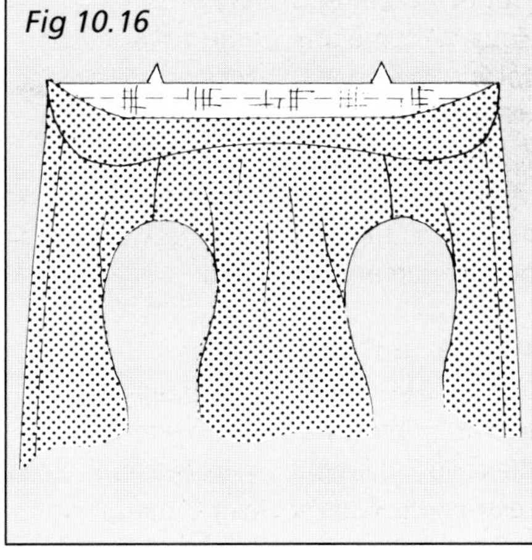

Fig 10.16 Take care not to catch in the free edge of the collar.

Fig 10.17

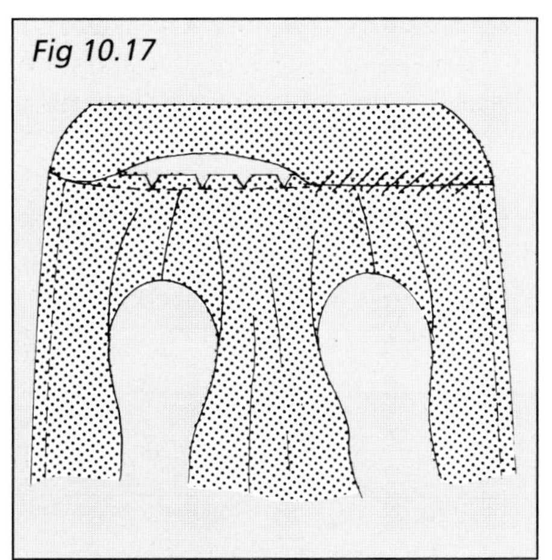

Fig 10.17 Hand-hem the folded edge on to the stitching line.

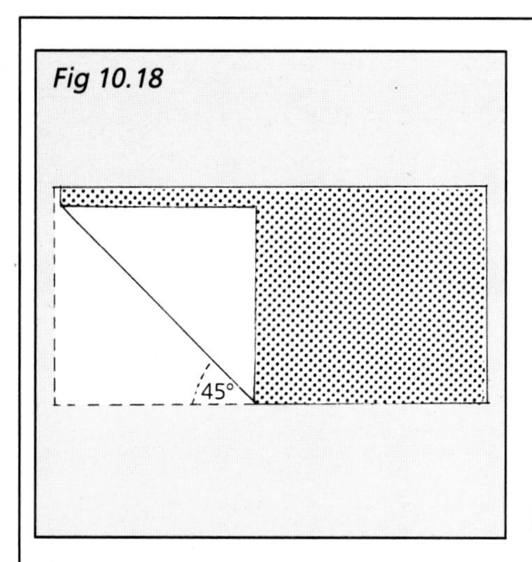

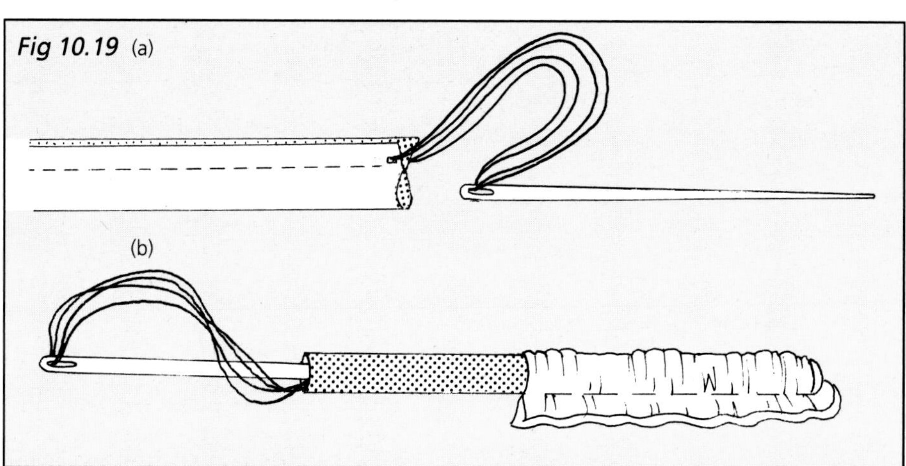

Fig 10.18 The cross-grain or bias of the fabric.

Fig 10.19 Turning the rouleau.

Fig 10.20 Attaching rouleaux.

ROULEAU LOOPS AND TIES

Stand collars are very often fastened at the neck with rouleau loops or ties. Rouleau ties are very narrow and unpressed to give a rounded appearance. They are cut on the bias, or cross-grain, of the fabric, that is at an angle of 45° from the selvage (Fig 10.18). The size of the strip you need to cut will be given above the cutting layout on your pattern.

Fold the strip in half lengthways and tack and stitch down the long side. Use a stretch-stitch on your machine if you have one. Trim the seam turning.

Attach a strong thread to one end of the tie and use it to thread a bodkin or large darning needle (Fig 10.19*a*). Insert the eye of the bodkin into the channel, easing the fabric along the thread to turn the tie right side out (Fig 10.19*b*).

Rouleau ties and single rouleau loops are made and inserted into the seam line before the facing is attached (Fig 10.20*a*). A close row of loops can be made by adding the rouleau in a continuous strip after the neck edge is complete (Fig 10.20*b*).

Rouleau loops should project beyond the edge of the facing by about two-thirds of the diameter of the button. Covered buttons look good with rouleau loops and these are simple to make following the manufacturer's instructions.

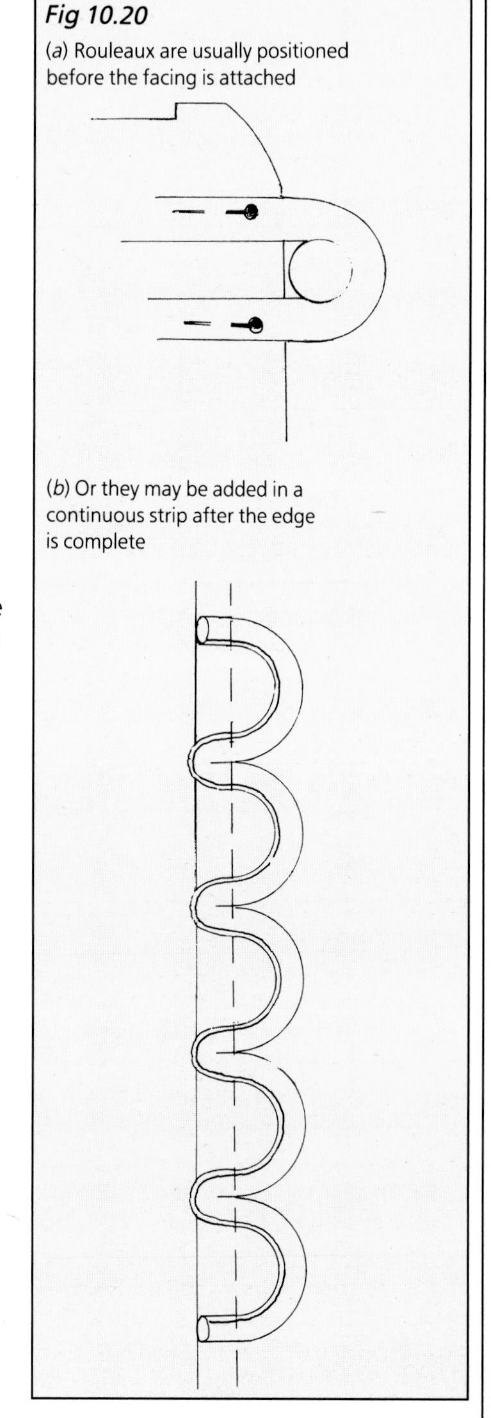

WAISTLINES

Once the neckline is finished, it is a good idea to tack the bodice and skirt together for a little basic fitting. Joining a skirt and top at the waistline is not a difficult procedure; it is just awkward, as there is so much fabric to handle.

Make sure that all gathers and pleats are tacked in *firmly*, and that the ends of any darts and seams in the bodice are stitched securely.

Turn the skirt wrong side out and the bodice right side out. Open out the top of the skirt and drop the bodice, neck edge first, inside the skirt. Match the side seams, centre front and back and any notches (Fig 10.21). Tack, using a small, firm tacking, along the marked seam line. Try on for fitting before stitching the waist seam.

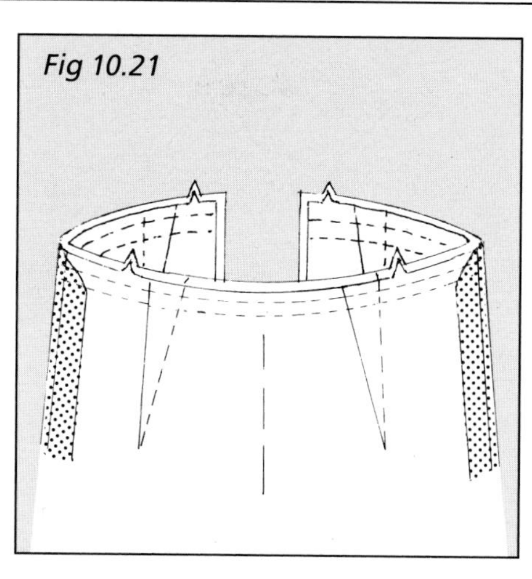

Fig 10.21 Match the side seams, centre front and back and any notches.

Fig 10.22 Larger seam allowances than usual at the waist can be turned up and stitched to form a casing.

Fig 10.23 Tack the bias binding over the casing line and stitch very close to both edges.

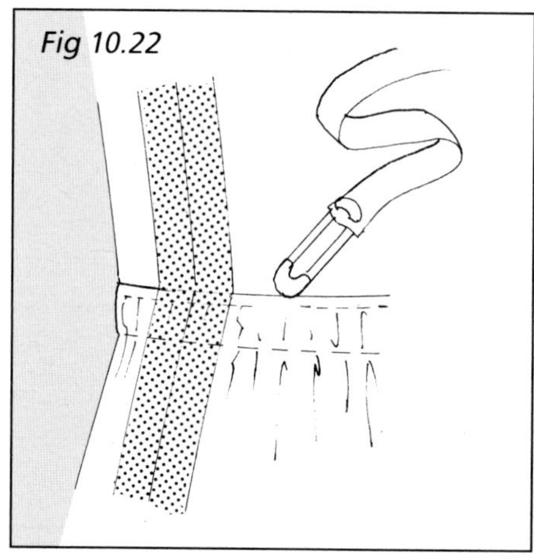

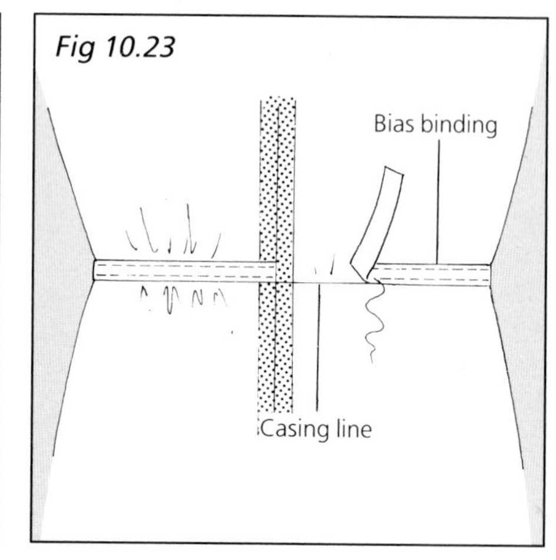

Elasticated waists
Many loosely fitting styles are held in at the waist with elastic. This is often achieved by taking a larger seam allowance at the waist than usual, then pressing both turnings up on to the bodice and stitching along them to form a casing (Fig 10.22).

If there is no waist seam, a separate casing is often stitched to the dress and a soft elastic threaded through to gather in the dress at the waist. Many dressmakers like to do this even on a dress which is designed to be held in at the waist with a belt and has no waist seam. The addition of a casing and elastic means that the fullness is held firmly and can be distributed more evenly than by using a belt only.

A casing can be made from a bias strip of self fabric or by using bias binding. If a casing line is marked on the dress, do not be too hasty in deciding that its position is too low for you. An allowance has often been made for the bodice to 'blouse over' at the waist.

If there is no line marked and you wish to add a casing, put the dress on inside-out, and use coloured tailor's chalk to chalk heavily on a length of string. Tie the string tightly round your waist, so that it leaves an imprint of chalk as a guide for the waistline casing.

Tack the bias binding over the casing line, right round the inside of the dress, starting and ending at a side seam. Stitch very close to both edges (Fig 10.23).

Insert soft elastic through the casing with a bodkin and adjust it to fit snugly. Oversew the ends of the elastic together. Oversew the opening in the casing. (But if your weight varies, it is a good idea to leave the casing open so that you can adjust it easily!)

BASIC FITTING

Fitting is not really something that can be taught. It is learned by trial and error! As you will have read in Lesson One, the difficulties of making clothes that fit are minimised by taking accurate measurements, choosing your correct pattern size, and adjusting the pattern length before you cut out. However, there may be minor adjustments from the standard sizes which will become apparent only when you try on the dress.

Tack as much of the dress together as you can. Tack the side seams, skirt panels or pleats, and the waist seam, but leave the sleeves out at this stage.

Put on the dress, fasten it correctly and stand in front of a full-length mirror. Start at the shoulders and check the following details.

The fit of the bodice Is it pulling over the bust because it is a little too tight, gaping at the underarm because it is too large, or is it a good, easy fit?

Adjustment here is made at the side seams. They can be let out or taken in as necessary. Any alteration must be divided equally between both side seams. Pin and tack the new side seam and then try on the dress again and do this several times until you are happy with the fit.

Bust darts should be in line with the fullest part of the bust. If they are not, move them up or down.

It is difficult to make these adjustments on yourself. It may help to put on the dress *wrong side out* to pin the alteration, but remember that the two sides of your body are not necessarily the same.

The fit of the waistline Put on a narrow belt with the dress. Is the dress waist in the same place as yours? Does the dress fit snugly at the waist or too tightly?

If the dress waist is not in the same place as yours, mark the position of the narrow belt with pins or chalk before removing the dress. When you have taken off the dress, take it apart at the waist. Adjust the side seams if necessary and retack the waist seam in the new position.

The fit of the shoulders If the dress is to have a set-in sleeve, does the shoulder width seem correct? If you are not happy with it, complete the making up and stitching of the dress as far as the sleeve, then refer to page 91 for adjusting the position of the shoulder and armhole line.

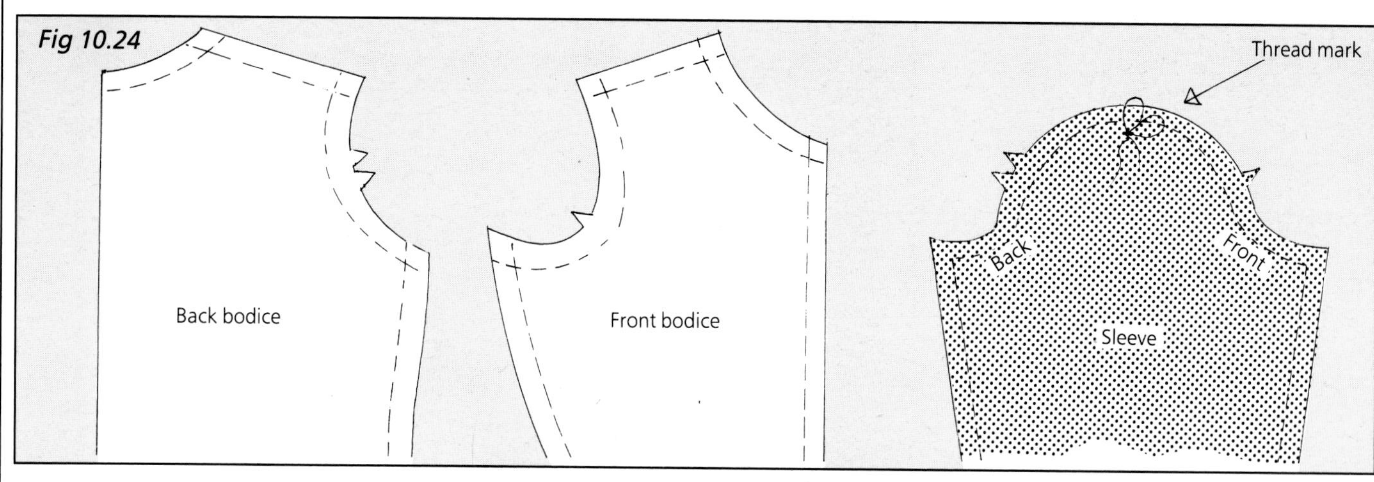

A GATHERED SLEEVE

Setting in a gathered sleeve

Have a look at your sleeve pieces and check that you have followed the instructions in Lesson Four and that you have the stitching lines marked, a thread mark at the sleeve head denoting the position for the shoulder seam and a single notch at the front and a double notch at the back of the sleeve (Fig 10.24).

First, stitch the sleeve seam and press it open. Lay the sleeves flat and you should have two corresponding sleeves, a right and a left (Fig 10.25). (It is always worth checking this if you have fabric which is the same on both sides, because it is all too easy to stitch up one on the wrong side, and end up with two sleeves for the same armhole!) The more hollowed out part of the sleeve is the front.

Work two rows of very small running stitches, starting at the front notch and working round the head of the sleeve to the back notch (Fig 10.26). Work one row just above the marked stitching line and the second line just below it. Start the stitching with a large knot and leave a long end. (Do not be tempted to take a short cut and do this stitching by machine. It is too tight and is not as easy to adjust as hand-stitching.)

With the bodice and the sleeve both right side out, position the sleeve with the seam to the underarm seam of the dress and pin the two seams exactly together. Working now from the inside of the dress – that is, looking *into* the sleeve – pin the sleeve into the armhole as far as the start of the gathers on both sides.

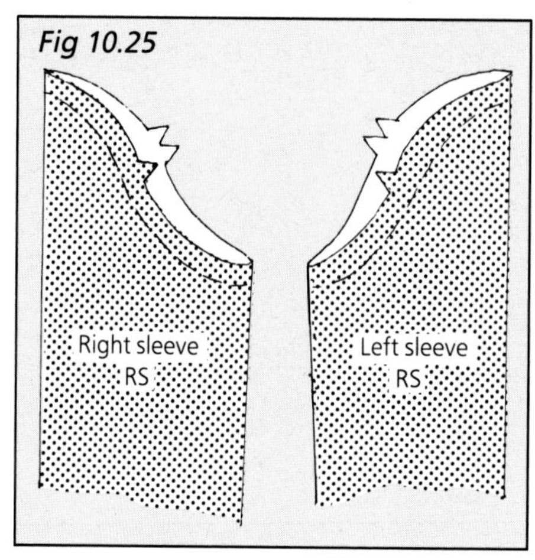

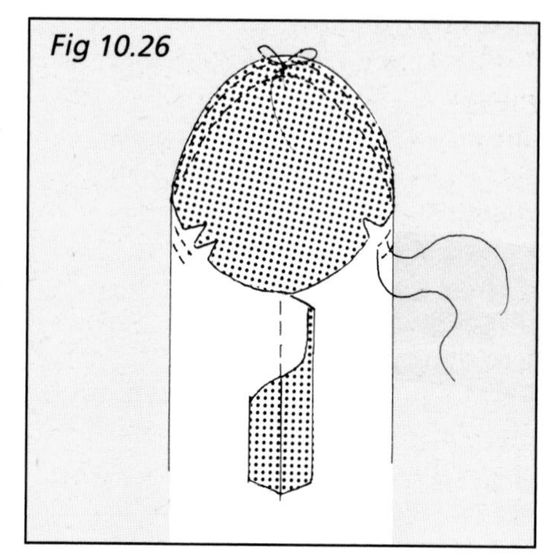

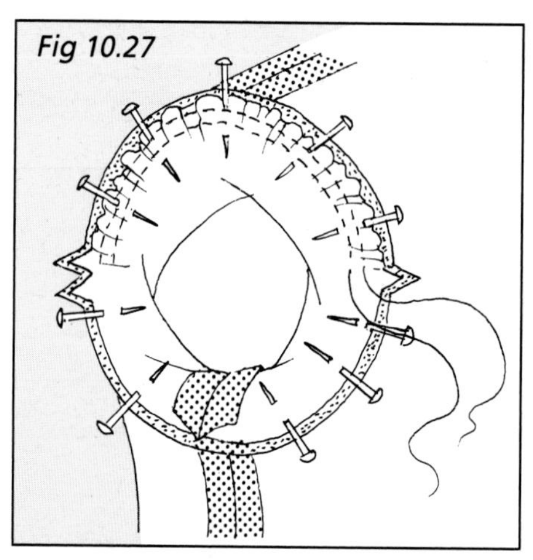

Pin the thread mark at the sleeve head to the shoulder seam. Draw up the gathers over the sleeve head with the long threads, easing the fullness to distribute it evenly. You will find it easier to do this if you fold the sleeve head over the curve of your hand with the gathers to the outside (Fig 10.27). Distribute the gathers evenly and tack round the armhole seam.

Fig 10.24 Make sure that you have the notches and stitching lines marked clearly.

Fig 10.25 Make sure that you have two corresponding sleeves, i.e. a left and a right.

Fig 10.26 Work two rows of very small running stitches round the head of the sleeve.

Fig 10.27 Distribute the gathers evenly, folding them over your hand to the outside.

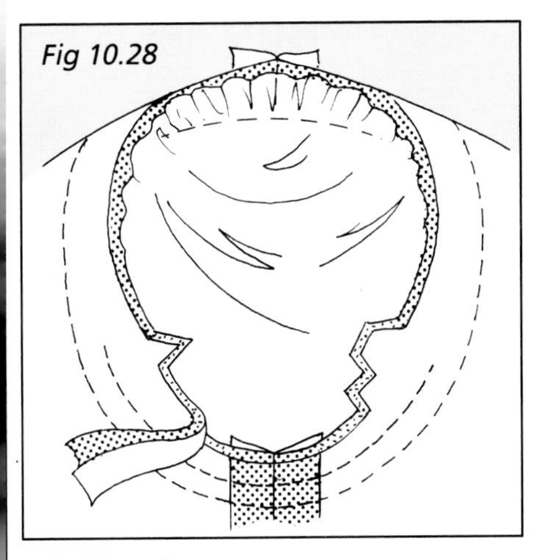

Stitching the seam
The best way to stitch in a sleeve is from the gathered side and *not* using the free arm on your machine, as this means stitching it with the flat side uppermost. (The free arm is ideal for other tasks, such as trouser legs, cuffs, etc.) With the gathered side uppermost, you can control the fullness and ensure that the gathers feed through evenly.

Stitch the sleeve with a small stitch; a stretch-stitch is ideal. Work a second row of stitching at the underarm to reinforce it. *Do not trim away any of the seam allowance over the sleeve head.* Trim the seam at the underarm only, to the second line of stitching (Fig 10.28).

A sleeve is very seldom improved by pressing. The turnings are not pressed open and they turn naturally into the sleeve head.

The sleeve hem
A sleeve hem on a dress is straightforward and is finished with a catch-stitch as described on page 43. If the sleeve is finished with a cuff, refer to pages 75–6.

Fig 10.28 Work a second row of stitching at the underarm to strengthen it, and trim the seam at the underarm only.

LESSON ELEVEN

Making a shirt blouse

You are now getting to grips with dressmaking. The making of a shirt-type blouse includes several important new techniques and when you have successfully mastered these, you can really call yourself a dressmaker, because by the end of this lesson you will have made considerable progress in dressmaking.

In this lesson you will learn to apply a shoulder yoke with neat top-stitching, tailor a shirt collar, make a cuff opening, apply a cuff and make buttonholes. When you add these techniques to those you have mastered in previous lessons, you will realise that you can now choose almost any pattern in the STYLE catalogue.

I say *almost* any pattern because at this stage we will omit a set-in sleeve. Most of the current shirt-type blouse patterns have easy-fitting armholes with a dropped shoulder line. These are straightforward to sew. Or you can choose a set-in sleeve with gathers over the sleeve head, which you learned in Lesson Ten. However, if you prefer a pattern in the classic style with the sleeve set in smoothly at the shoulder, you can jump ahead for that technique and refer to setting in a sleeve on pages 88–90.

So leaf through the STYLE catalogue and enjoy choosing a blouse pattern with buttons, instead of avoiding them as most beginners have to do. Choose a shirt-type collar and a cuffed sleeve, referring again to the lessons on choosing your pattern and your fabric.

When you cut out your blouse, you will find that there are more pattern pieces than for a skirt or top. Follow the routine for cutting out on pages 18–20, paying special attention to the list of things to watch out for, as your blouse will no doubt include some of these variations on the cutting layout.

The blouse front pattern has a great deal of information on it which you *must* transfer accurately with thread marking on to the fabric. As you will have done before, use different colours of thread for this, and write down on your pattern envelope what each colour signifies: for instance, buttonholes – blue; pockets – brown; fold line – white; centre line – red.

When a blouse or dress has a front opening, the centre lines are extremely important: they are placed on top of each other when the garment is fitted and give the correct balance for each side, so that you know how much to overlap the two fronts. It is a good idea always to use the same colour for the centre line whatever you make, so that it is easily identified. Bright red is the ideal colour. If you keep a red thread in your workbox for this, you can also use it to mark the most important notch on the sleeve pattern, which is the notch which marks the sleeve head – the place where the sleeve joins the shoulder seam of the blouse – and balances the sleeve so that it hangs straight.

If you keep to red for these vital balance marks – centre lines on the blouse fronts (and on the collar when they occur) and the notch on the sleeve head – you can check at a glance where the pieces relate.

The shirt pattern you have chosen will almost certainly have pockets, and this is the first unit to make up and attach while the blouse fronts are flat. Refer back to Lesson Nine for help with the pockets. If the design you have chosen has pocket flaps, these need to be interfaced with a lightweight interfacing. The blouse fronts are then joined to the back, usually by means of a yoke.

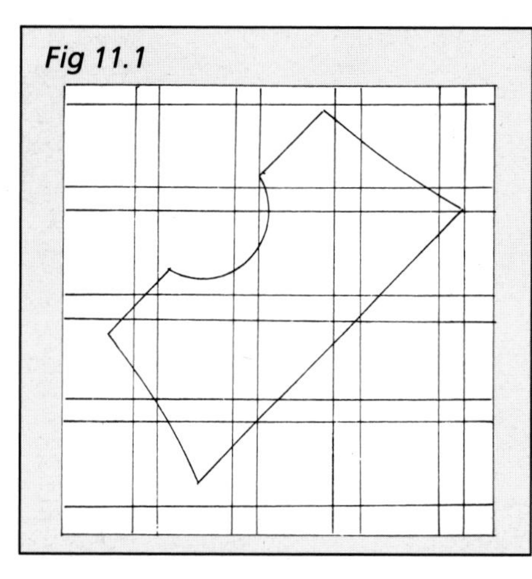

Fig 11.1 Cut both yokes on the cross on checked fabric.

Fig 11.2 Place the gathered or pleated back piece on top of the yoke.

Fig 11.3 Machine-stitch through all three thicknesses.

Fig 11.4 Stitch the fronts to the front edges of the top yoke only.

Fig 11.5 Bring the folded edge on to the stitching line and hem in place.

A SHOULDER YOKE

A yoke gives a very tailored look to a blouse, as the shoulder seams are set to the front and the back, instead of on top of the shoulder. A yoke is best made double: the inside lining yoke conceals all the raw edges and also gives a firm shoulder which keeps its shape.

You will find that the yoke pattern states CUT TWO for a lined yoke so that the two shapes are identical. If your pattern does not suggest a double yoke, it is still better to cut two and adapt it yourself into a lined yoke.

If you are using a checked fabric, cut both yokes on the cross; this looks attractive and does away with the need to match the checks (Fig 11.1).

A yoke fits smoothly over the shoulders and the fabric of the front and back pieces is fuller to give a loose, bloused effect. This fabric is pleated or gathered in to fit the yoke. Mark the section to be drawn up carefully, and cut the notches on the yoke and the corresponding notches on the front and back accurately. For help with gathering and pleating fabric, see pages 30–2.

Attaching the yoke

First, determine which is the *back* edge of the yoke. Place one yoke piece, right side uppermost, flat on the table, with the back edge furthest away from you. Place the gathered or pleated back piece on top, wrong side uppermost, with the raw edges together and the notches matched (Fig 11.2). Pin, with the pins at right angles to the edge.

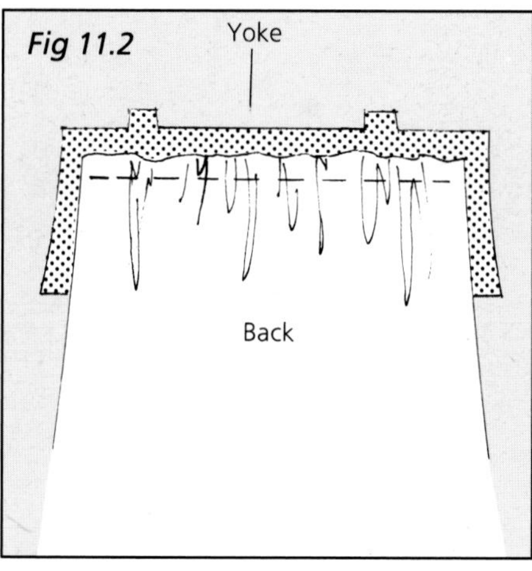

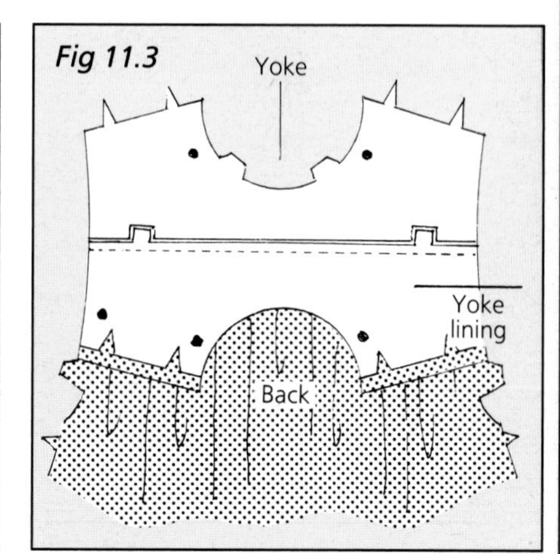

Place the second yoke piece, which now becomes the *yoke lining*, wrong side uppermost on the top of the yoke, matching the notches as before and enclosing the edge of the yoke. Pin as before and tack and machine along the stitching line, through all three thicknesses (Fig 11.3).

Press both yoke pieces away from the back. When pressing any straight edge joined to a gathered section, you will find it a help to place the flat section, in this case the yoke back, right on the edge of the ironing board, allowing the gathers to fall free over the edge to avoid flattening them.

With the right sides together, stitch the front blouse pieces to the front edges of the *top yoke only*, as above, leaving the yoke lining free (Fig 11.4). Press the seam towards the yoke and bring over the yoke lining to enclose the raw edges. Press under the seam allowance on the loose edge of the yoke lining. Bring this folded edge down on to the stitching line, tack and hem in place (Fig 11.5).

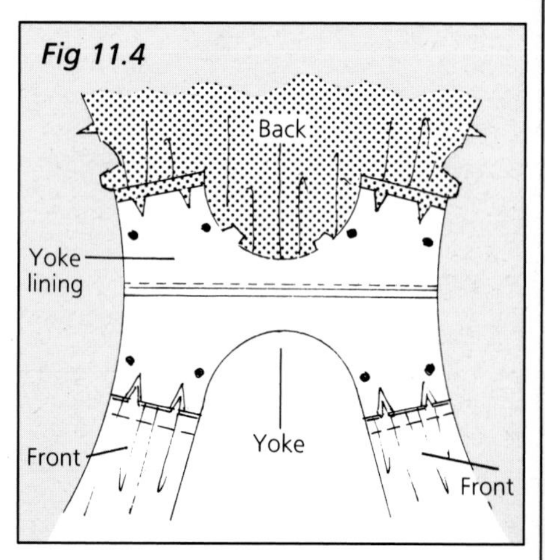

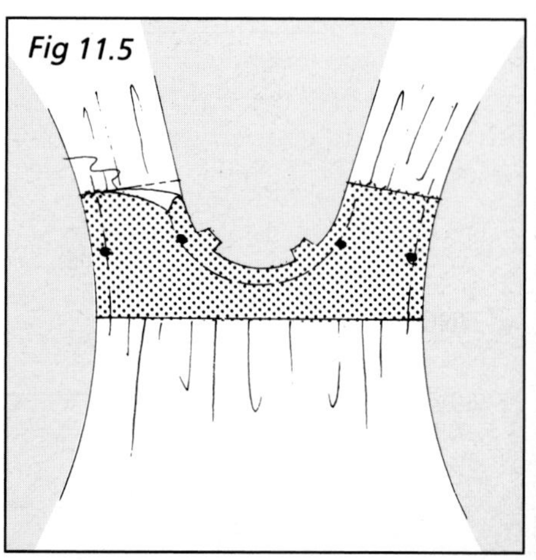

TOP-STITCHING

A yoke is improved by bold top-stitching. Top-stitching is a line of bold stitching for decorative purposes. It must be done as you complete a unit, rather than after you have finished the shirt.

There are several ways to top-stitch a garment, but the important thing is that the stitching must be absolutely straight, with an even stitch, whichever method you use. You may have a seam guide attachment for your machine which will help you. But to make things really easy for yourself, take time to stitch a guideline, by hand, in a contrasting colour, exactly on the line you wish to top-stitch. Measure in from the edge – 6mm (¼ in) is usual for a shirt, but up to 1.2 cm (½ in) looks better on heavy fabric – and work along the edges and round the curves with a long stitch, through the top layer of fabric only (Fig 11.6).

Then, top-stitch over the guideline and, if you are a complete beginner with your sewing machine, top-stitch in a thread which is a fairly good match with your fabric, so that it will not be too noticeable for your first attempt! When you have had some practice at sewing, you might like to try the following suggestions.

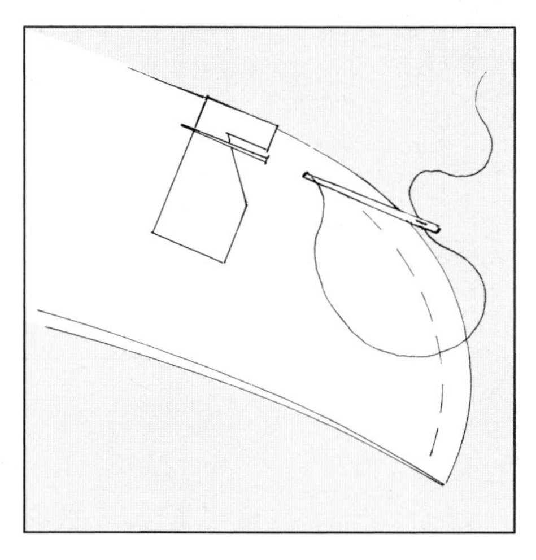

Fig 11.6 Tack to mark the top-stitching line.

Variations on top-stitching

Threads There are several threads on the market made specifically for top-stitching. They are thicker than usual with a raised appearance to give strong top-stitched lines. Some also have a superb sheen. You may need to change the needle in your machine to a number 16, which has a larger eye, to use these threads. Thread the needle in the bold stitch thread and thread the spool with the normal thread. Stitch, with the machine set at the longest stitch.

Experiment with the colour of the top-stitching thread. Shades slightly darker than the fabric or even a complete contrast can look effective. With a shiny thread, a shade lighter than the fabric looks good.

Twin-needle stitching Most machines will take a twin needle. This is a double needle on a single shank. The shank fits most machines and many machines offer this as a standard accessory. Thread up the machine in the usual way with two reels of thread, separating the threads at the needle with one through each eye. The spool is threaded in the usual way. Stitch along the marked line with a twin needle, to give two neat parallel rows of stitching.

Stretch-stitching The triple stretch-stitch on your machine is ideal for top-stitching as each stitch is made three times, giving a bold line.

Embroidery stitches If you have embroidery stitches on your machine, some of the narrower geometric patterns look effective as top-stitching.

When to top-stitch

All shirt styles, that is blouses and shirt-waister dresses, are improved with dominant top-stitching and so are most collars, cuffs and pocket edges in plain fabrics.

Checked and patterned fabrics do not need dominant top-stitching but often need a line of stitching to keep the edges crisp. In this case, top-stitch the edges using a small stitch and a very good match of a fine thread. This will give an inconspicuous top-stitching.

Top-stitch the yoke before moving on to deal with the front facings.

FRONT FACINGS

The front facings of a shirt blouse are sometimes cut as one with the front and folded to the inside, or they are cut as a separate facing piece which is stitched to the front and then turned to the inside. In both cases, the front facings are strengthened with interfacing, as are the collar and the cuffs. For help with choosing and applying interfacing, see Lesson Nine.

Interface the front facings and attach them if they are cut separately, and next, *before* the side seams are joined, deal with the collar.

A SHIRT COLLAR

If you follow all the exhortations you have been given to be accurate and prolific with your thread markings, putting on a shirt collar is a very satisfying job: it looks so professional when it is finished!

Making up the collar

A shirt collar needs to be stiffened with the correct weight of interfacing, and this is one instance where you might prefer a slightly heavier interfacing than usual. Apply the interfacing to one side of the collar following the instructions given on page 58, and then draw the *exact* shape of the collar in pencil on the interfacing. This gives you the exact stitching line, so that the shape, the corners or curves and the size of the collar in relation to the neck of the blouse are correct and you will have no problem fitting the two together.

Tack and stitch the two collar pieces together, round the outside edges.

Trim down the seam turnings to 6 mm (1/4 in). Then cut *one* seam edge away a little more. *Layering the seam edges* like this helps to prevent a ridge round the collar edge, especially in a thick fabric. Cut off the corners close to the stitching line (Fig 11.7).

Turn the collar right side out, ease out the corners, and edge-tack. Edge-tacking was illustrated in Lesson Nine and it is a vital stage for a really good finish to any collar. Work the seam between the finger and thumb and tack exactly on the edge, using a small stitch, to hold the edge in place.

Press the collar three times, first on the right side, using a steam iron or hot iron and damp cloth, then on the wrong side, and then again on the right side to remove any imprint of the tacking.

Top-stitch the collar in the same way as the yoke (Fig 11.8).

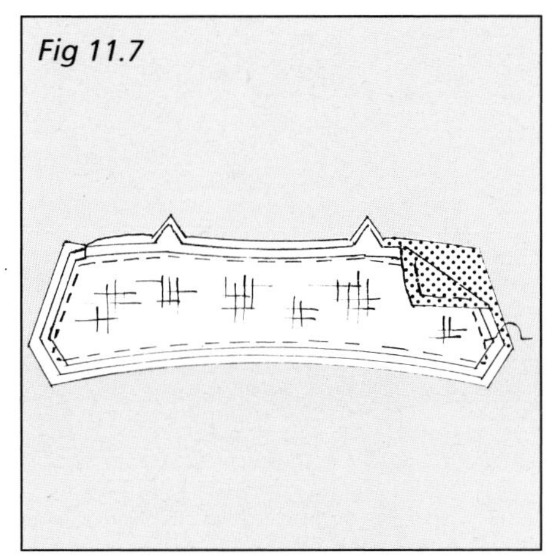
Fig 11.7

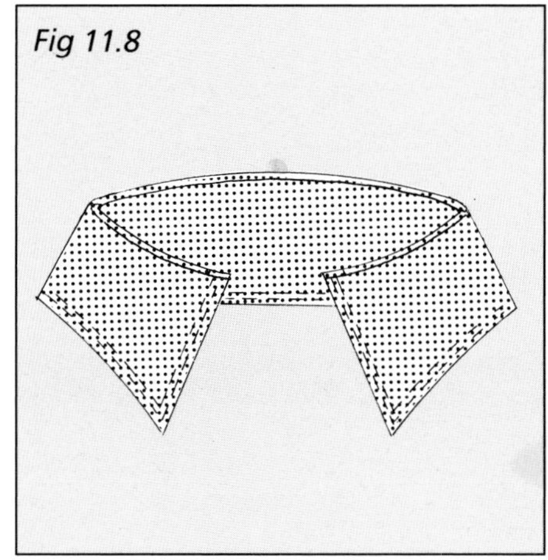
Fig 11.8

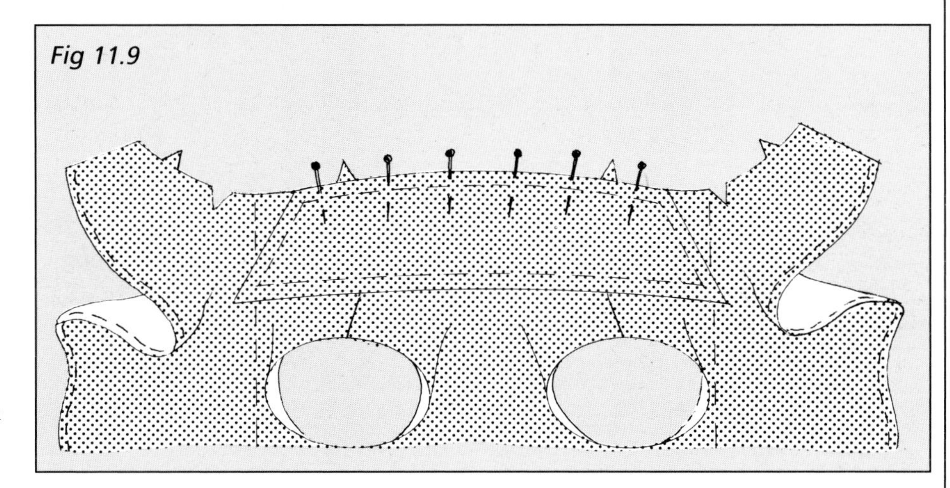
Fig 11.9

Attaching a shirt collar

Place the blouse right side uppermost on the table. Clip the curve of the neck edge almost to the line of stay-stitching. Ease it out into less of a curve and more of a straight line.

Place the collar, interfaced side down, to the neck edge, raw edges together. First, match the centre front lines at each end and pin these together, inserting the pins vertically. Match the shoulder marks and pin. Ease the collar to fit, matching the remaining notches and keeping the marked seam lines together, and pin (Fig 11.9).

Fold back the facing, on the fold line, over the collar. Check the mark on the collar which denotes the position of the end of the facing. Remove the facing. Snip through all thicknesses at that mark. Tack the collar to the blouse from the collar edge to the snip. Fold back the open edge of the *top* collar piece and continue tacking the rest of the neck edge through the interfaced under-collar and blouse only (Fig 11.10).

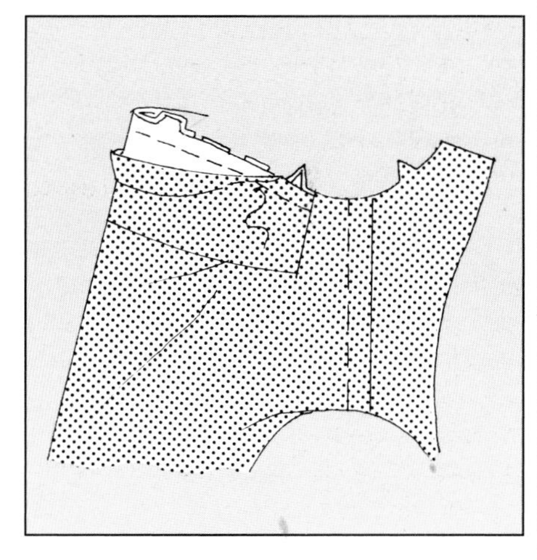

Fig 11.7 Layer the seam and cut off the corners close to the stitching line.

Fig 11.8 Top-stitch the collar.

Fig 11.9 Match the notches, keeping the seam allowance lines together, and pin.

Fig 11.10 Between the snips, tack the rest of the neck edge through the under-collar and blouse only.

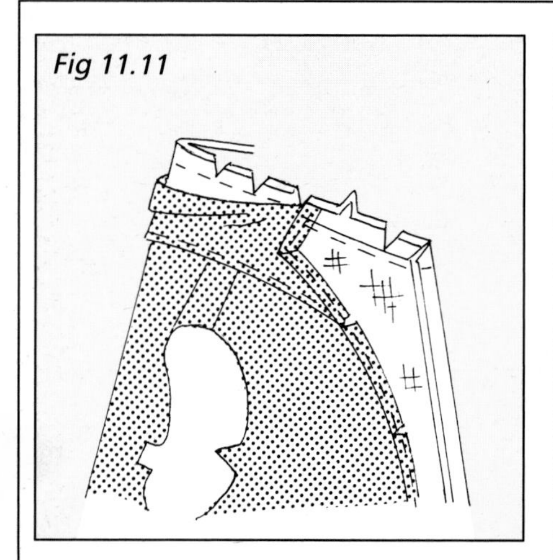

Fig 11.11 Stitch along the seam line, taking care not to catch in the free edge of the collar.

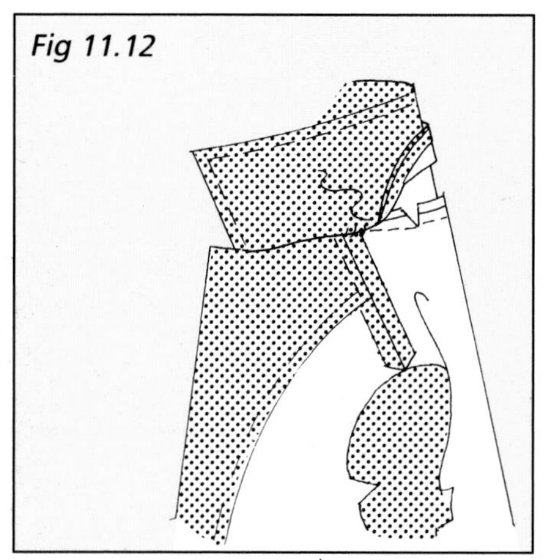

Fig 11.12 Hem the open edge in place on to the stitching line.

Turn the facing to the outside once more on the fold line, over the collar, and tack in place. Stitch along the seam line, taking care not to catch in the free edge of the collar (Fig 11.11).

Trim the seam to 6 mm (¼ in). Cut off the corners and turn the facing to the inside. Press. Press the seam at the back neck upwards, inside the collar. Turn under the marked seam allowance on the open edge of the collar, and tack and hem it in place on to the stitching line (Fig 11.12).

A shirt collar band

Sometimes, a shirt collar is cut a little smaller and given a separate collar band to support it.

A proper shirt with a collar band may also have a front band, similar to a man's shirt, rather than a front facing. This band must also be interfaced and stitched on to the front edge, turned and finished before the collar and collar band are attached.

Make up and top-stitch the collar as before. Tack the open edges of the collar together (Fig 11.13).

Interface one of the band pieces. Open out the neck edge and proceed as above, tacking the band, right sides together, to the neck edge, and matching the centre lines, notches and other markings. Stitch along the marked seam line. Trim the seam and clip the curves. Press the band upwards and press the seam towards the band (Fig 11.14).

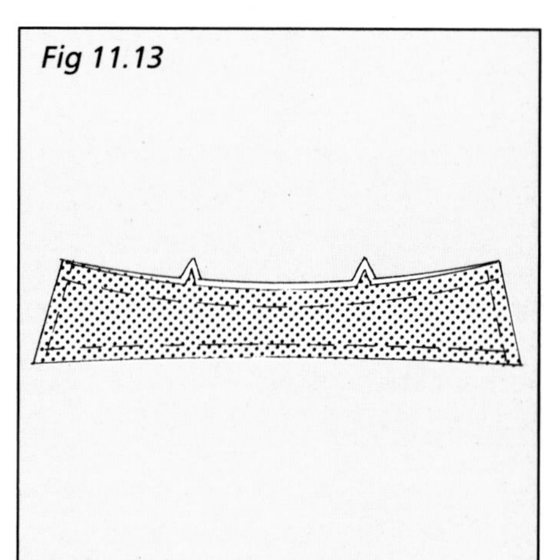

Fig 11.13 Tack the open edges of the collar together.

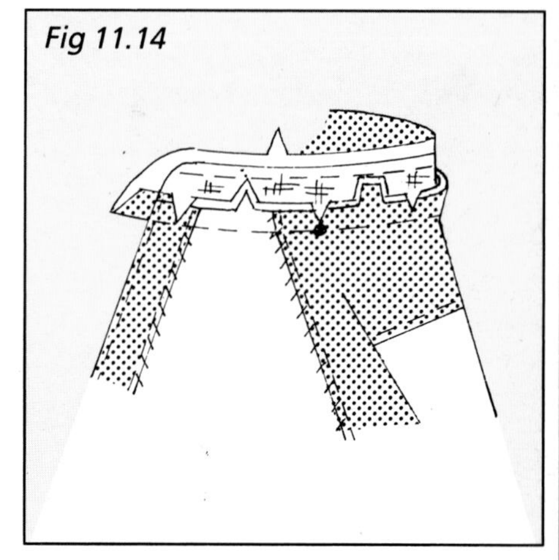

Fig 11.14 Press the band upwards and press the seam towards the band.

Place the *interfaced side* of the collar against the neck band, with the raw edges together, matching the notches and markings and pin and tack along the seam line (Fig 11.15).

Turn under the seam allowance on the straight edge of the other collar band. Place this band, right sides together, over the first band, enclosing the collar. Tack and stitch along the seam line (Fig 11.16). Trim the seam and clip the curves almost to the stitching line.

Turn the band to the right side and press it. (The collar should already have had its final pressing, so slip the band to the end of the ironing board, allowing the collar to hang free over the edge to avoid creasing.) Bring the loose edge of the band down on to the seam line, and tack and hem it in place (Fig 11.17).

Top-stitch the collar band in the same way as the collar (Fig 11.18).

SHIRT SLEEVES

The shirt sleeves are attached next. With the dropped sleeve line, this is simply a straight seam. After stitching, press the seam towards the neck edge and top-stitch (Fig 11.19).

The side and underarm seams are then joined in one. To give a neat and traditional finish to a shirt, you might like to finish the seams as *felled seams*.

A felled seam

A felled seam is a neat, flat seam with the raw edges enclosed and top-stitched. First, stitch the seam with the *wrong sides* together. Press both seam allowances in the same direction. Trim the underneath seam allowance down to 3 mm (⅛ in). Turn under the remaining seam allowance to 6 mm (¼ in), tack and edge-stitch to the garment (Fig 11.20).

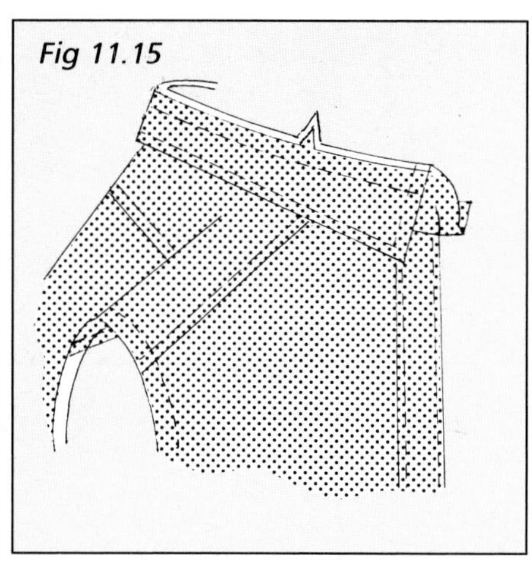

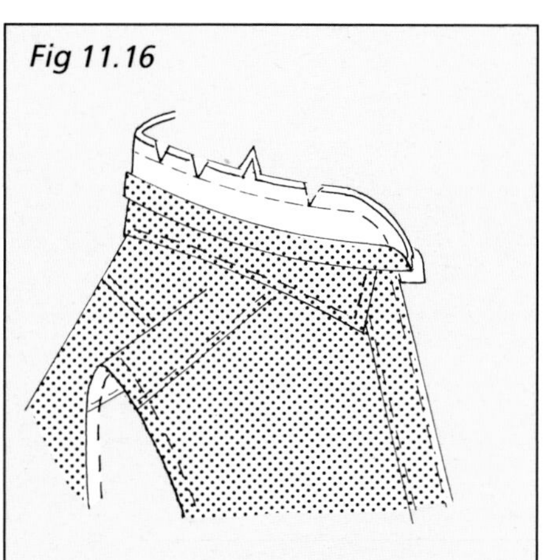

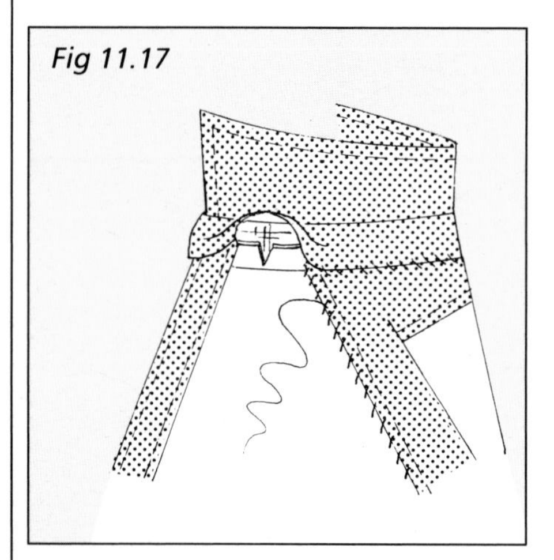

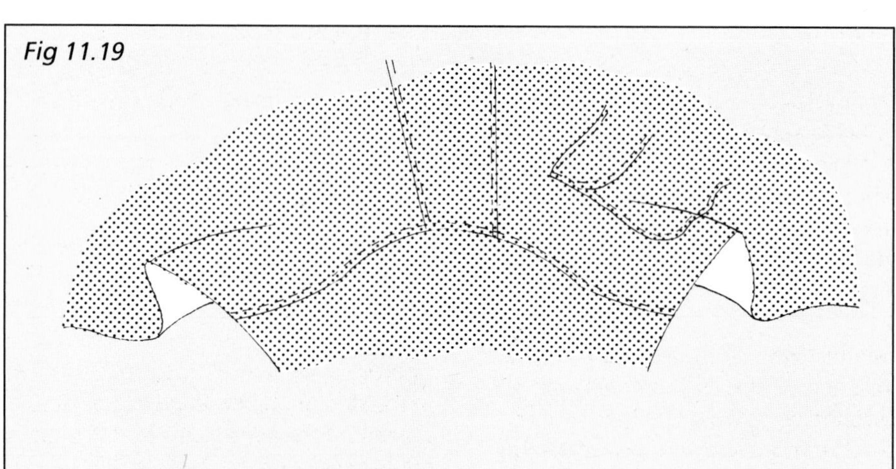

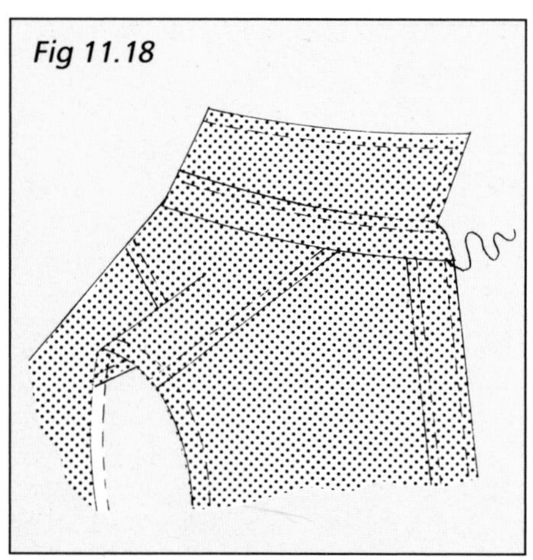

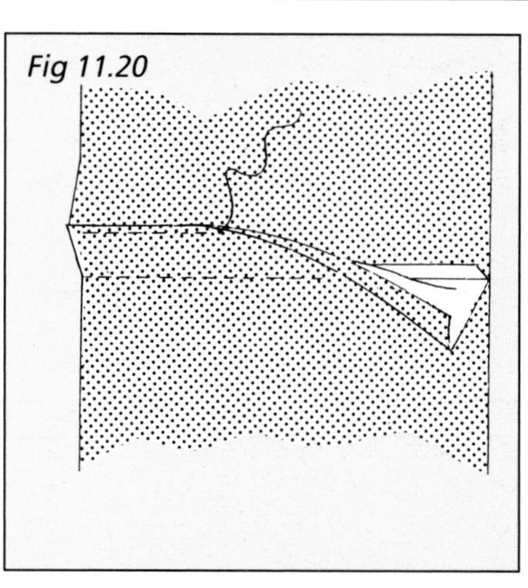

Fig 11.15 Place the collar on to the band and tack along the seam line.

Fig 11.16 Trim the seam and clip the curves almost to the stitching line.

Fig 11.17 Hem the loose edge of the band on to the seam line.

Fig 11.18 Top-stitch the collar band.

Fig 11.19 Press the shirt sleeve seam towards the neck edge and top-stitch.

Fig 11.20 A felled seam.

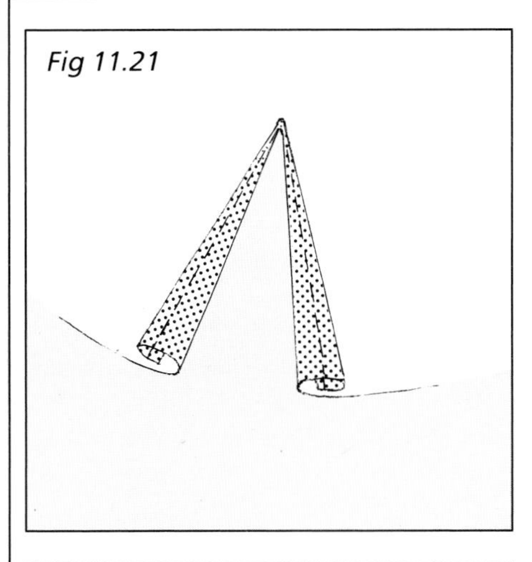

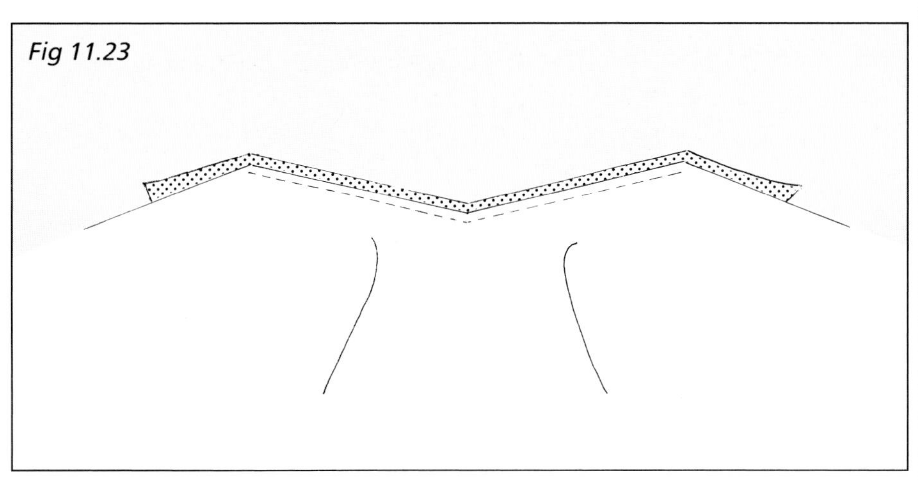

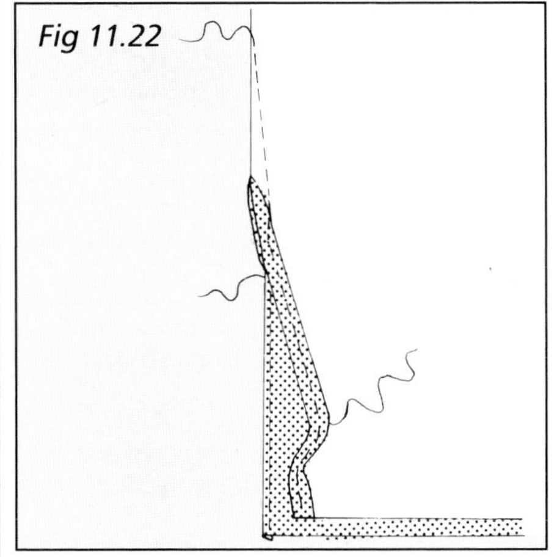

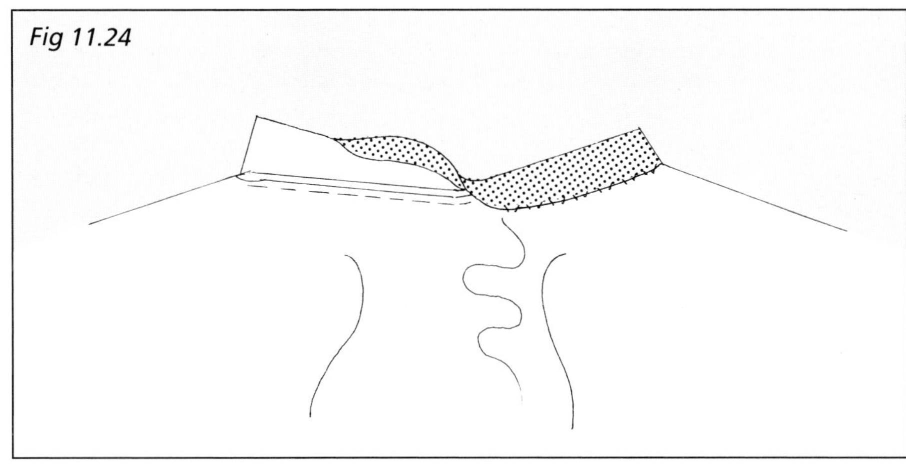

Shirt cuffs

A simple cuff opening

Making a shirt cuff opening used to be the kind of procedure it was worth choosing short sleeves to avoid! But recent STYLE patterns adopt this delightfully easy way of neatening a shirt cuff opening.

Slit the sleeve on the line marked for the opening. Turn a very narrow hem to the wrong side on both raw edges (Fig 11.21). This leaves an untidy end at the top of the opening. To neaten, fold the narrow hems together, right sides inside. Starting about 1.2 cm (½ in) down from the end of the opening, tack and stitch close to the edge, continuing the tacking for the same amount beyond the opening and tapering to a fine point, to form a small dart (Fig 11.22). Press the dart.

A faced cuff opening

Cuff openings may also be neatened with a facing. The procedure is the same as that described for the faced neck opening on page 55, but no interfacing is added.

A continuous lap opening

This is the name given to an opening neatened with one continuous strip of fabric.

Cut the strip to the size given. (If there is no separate pattern piece for the strip, the suggested size will be given above the cutting layout.) Cut the opening on the marked line.

Open out the slit, and place one long side of the strip to the raw edge, right sides together. Tack and machine-stitch close to the edge, with the sleeve side uppermost, and avoid catching in the fullness (Fig 11.23).

Press the strip away from the slit. Press under a narrow turning on the raw edge of the strip. Fold the strip in half so that the folded edge lies on top of the machine-stitching. Hand-hem in place (Fig 11.24).

Press the lap to the inside of the sleeve, and stitch diagonally across the top, to hold it in place (Fig 11.25).

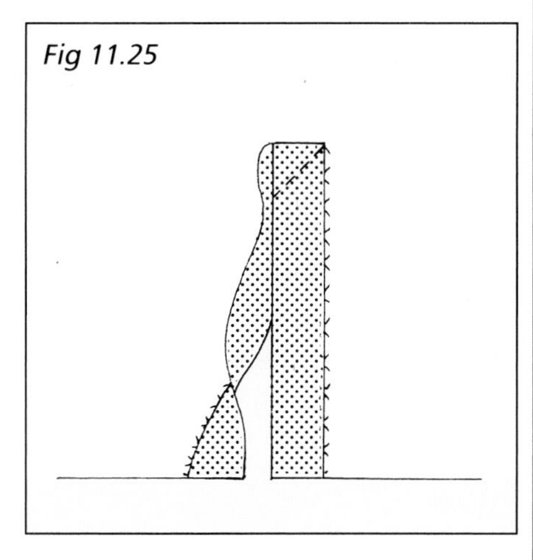

Fig 11.21 Turn a narrow hem on the raw edges.

Fig 11.22 Form a small dart at the end.

Fig 11.23 Machine close to the edge.

Fig 11.24 Hand-hem the folded edge on to the machine stitching.

Fig 11.25 Stitch diagonally across the top.

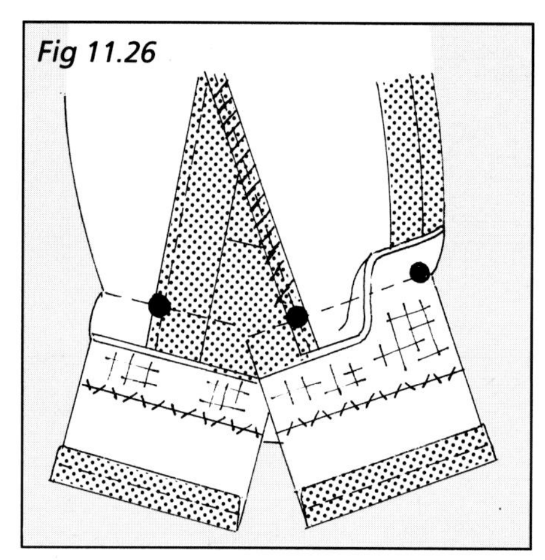

Attaching the cuff

The easiest time to attach the cuff is *before* you stitch the ends.

Gather or pleat the edge of the sleeve, according to the pattern instructions. (For help with gathering and forming pleats, see pages 30–2.)

Make sure that you have all the markings and notches marked correctly on the cuff pieces. Interface the cuff with the same type of interfacing used for the collar.

Press under the seam allowance on the long unnotched side of the cuff, to the wrong side. With the right sides together, pin the other side to the sleeve edge, matching the notches and markings. Tack and stitch along the marked seam line (Fig 11.26).

Trim the seam turnings to 6 mm (¼ in). Fold the cuff along the marked fold line, *right* sides together, and stitch across the ends (Fig 11.27). Trim the seams and cut off the corners. Turn the cuff to the right side, edge-tack the ends and the fold line, and press.

Bring the open edge of the cuff down on to the stitching line and hem in place (Fig 11.28).

If the cuff has an overlap which projects beyond the opening, turn under the raw edges and slip-stitch the edges together (Fig 11.29).

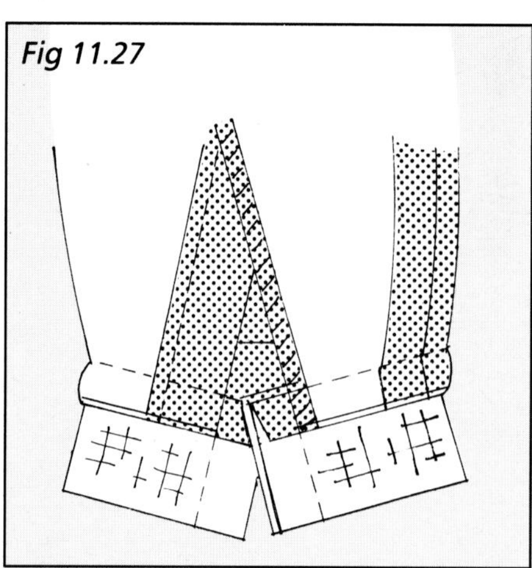

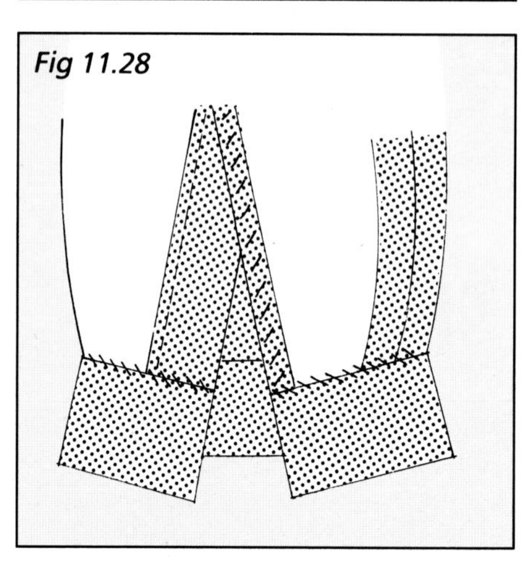

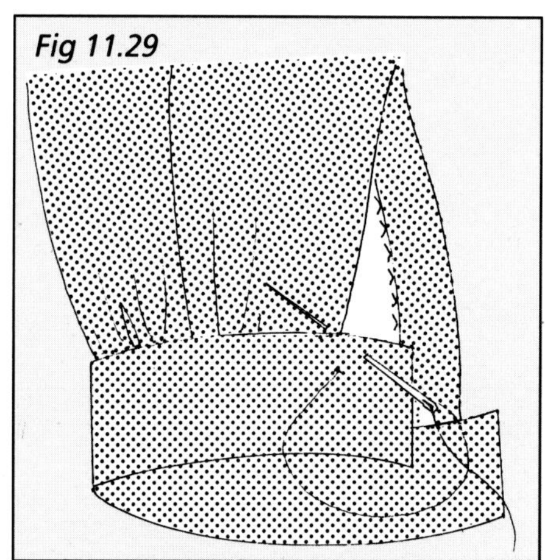

Fig 11.26 Attaching the cuff to the sleeve edge.

Fig 11.27 Stitch the ends of the cuff.

Fig 11.28 Hem the inside of the cuff.

Fig 11.29 Slip-stitch the overlap.

Fig 11.30 Marking the positions for the buttonholes.

Fig 11.31 Machine round the cutting line of the buttonhole.

Fig 11.32 Insert the needle just below the line of machine stitching.

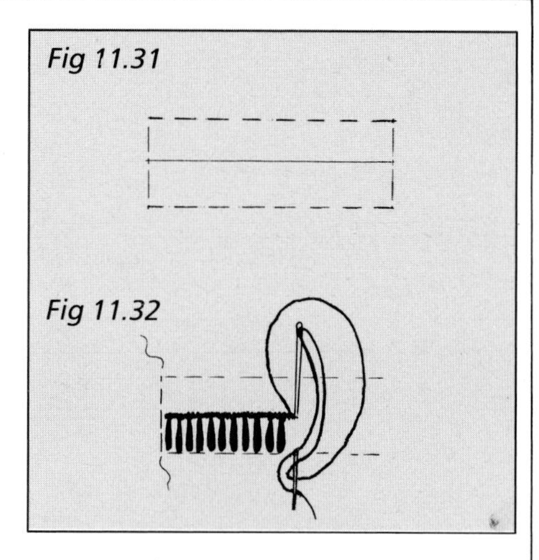

BUTTONHOLES

There is no way out with buttonholes! They just have to be done. But there are several ways in which you can make the task easier. They do not make it any quicker – in fact, they are small additional stages – but they *will* simplify it for you.

Marking the position for the buttonholes

Marking the position for the buttons and buttonholes *exactly* is the first thing to simplify the task. The buttons are always stitched *on* the centre front line. (Which, of course, is already clearly marked with a red thread!) *Horizontal buttonholes* are positioned over the centre line, with three-quarters of their length towards the side seam and one-quarter towards the front edge of the garment. This means that, when the blouse is fastened and the shank of the button is in place, the centre front lines lie on top of one another, which is correct. *Vertical buttonholes* are placed *on* the centre line.

Although your pattern gives a general guide for the position of the buttonholes, you have to take into account your figure, any pattern alteration and the button size, if any of these is not the same as the pattern suggests. Position the first buttonhole at the fullest part of the bust, to prevent gaping, and adjust the other buttons evenly, up and down. Check the position of the top button, according to how you will wear the collar, and check the position of the waist button in relation to a belt.

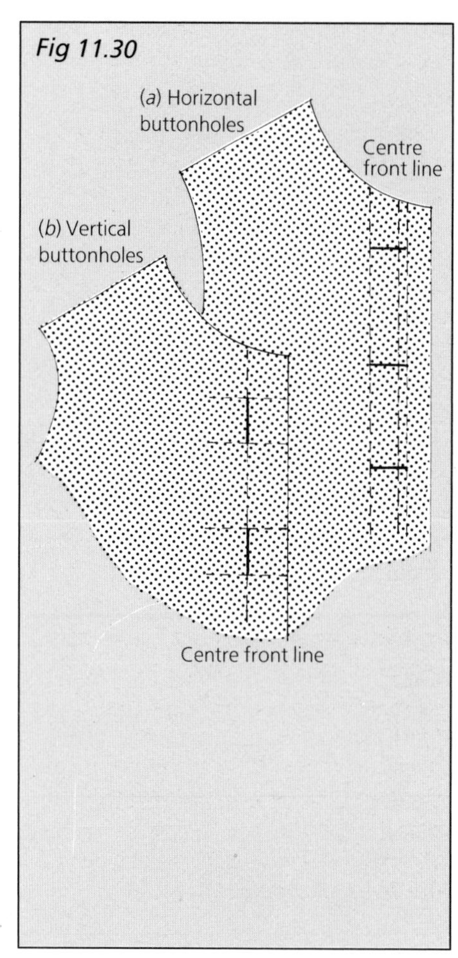

The clearest way to mark the exact position for horizontal buttonholes is to tack two lines parallel to the centre front line on the right front. Make these lines the width of the finished buttonhole. At the position of the buttonhole, stitch a line across between the two vertical lines (Fig 11.30).

The length of your buttonhole is the diameter of the button plus 3 mm (⅛ in).

A hand-worked buttonhole

Buttonholes on very fine fabrics are best made by hand. People who enjoy hand sewing prefer to make buttonholes this way and if you have just a basic sewing machine, you have no choice anyway.

First, reinforce the wrong side of the buttonhole area by inserting a small strip of Wundaweb fusible fleece between the facing and the blouse front to cover the cutting line. Press, using a damp cloth, so that the fabric of the blouse and the facing are fused together at the buttonhole. This reinforces the area, making the buttonhole easier to handle and the cut edge firmer for stitching.

Machine-stitch using a small stitch on each side of the marked line for the buttonhole and 3 mm (⅛ in) away from it (Fig 11.31). Cut the buttonhole along the marked cutting line.

Work the buttonhole from left to right, beginning at the inner left-hand edge (in other words, nearest the side seam). Insert the needle into the back of the work and bring out the thread at the edge of the slit. Insert the needle just below the line of machine stitching and bring the double end of the thread round and under the point of the needle (Fig 11.32). Ease the thread through to form a knot. The stitch should be upright and the knot should be eased to lie exactly on the cut edge.

Work along the buttonhole edge in this way, making sure the stitches are upright and the thickness of the thread apart.

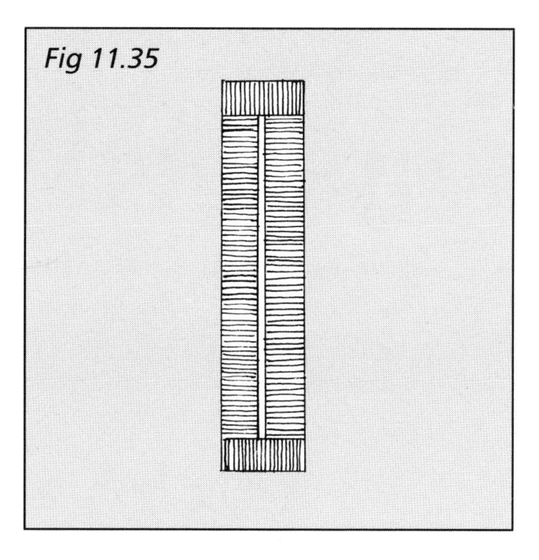

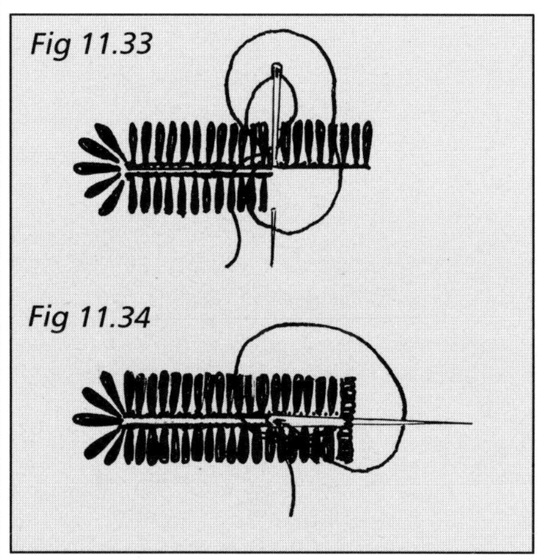

At the right-hand edge of the buttonhole nearest the centre front, fan out the stitches, taking 5–7 stitches round the end (Fig 11.33). Turn the work so that you continue to work from left to right in buttonhole stitch along the other edge.

Finish the other end of the buttonhole with a bar tack. Take four stitches across the end to give four threads lying together. Insert the *eye* of the needle under these threads with the single thread underneath the eye as the needle is pulled through, giving a blanket stitch (Fig 11.34). Work along the bar easing the stitches very close together. Take the thread through to the back of the fabric and work a bar on the back in the same way. Press the buttonhole.

Vertical buttonholes are worked with two bar ends (Fig 11.35).

Machine buttonholes

It is even more important to mark the position of the buttonholes accurately if you are stitching them by machine, as picking out a machine buttonhole is not fun!

Study your machine handbook. It depends on the type of machine you have whether you have to adjust the satin stitch yourself, or whether the machine has a pre-set buttonhole stitch. Either way, make several practice buttonholes on the same thickness of fabric and interfacing and, when you make a start on the blouse front, begin with the lower buttonholes (which, if necessary, can be tucked into a skirt!).

Machine buttonholes are worked and then cut. Use sharp embroidery scissors or a 'quick-unpick' (the cutting tool for unpicking machine stitching) to cut the buttonhole. Insert a pin at one end of the buttonhole, just in front of the bar tack. Insert the point of the quick-unpick just behind the other bar tack and slit the buttonhole to the pin (Fig 11.36).

Finish the hem of your shirt blouse as explained in Lesson Eight.

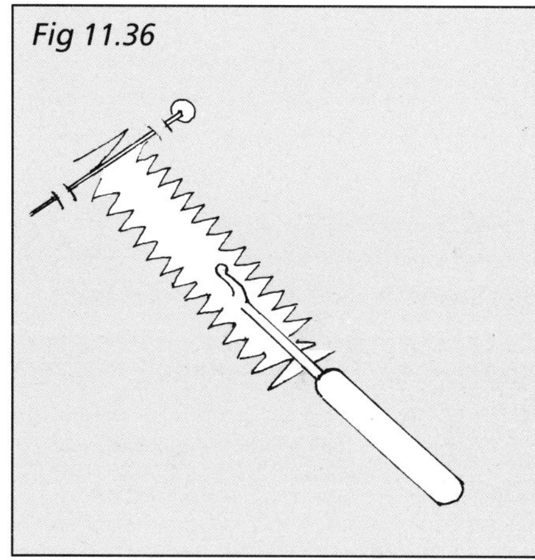

Fig 11.33 Buttonhole and end stitches.

Fig 11.34 Working a bar at the end of a buttonhole.

Fig 11.35 Vertical buttonholes are worked with two bar ends.

Fig 11.36 Slit the buttonhole to the pin.

LESSON TWELVE

Making an unlined jacket

Now that you have successfully made a shirt blouse and a dress, making an unlined jacket is well within your scope. In fact, you may find making a jacket is simpler because the fabric is heavier and easier to work with.

An unlined jacket is now all you need to complement the wardrobe of clothes you have made during these sewing lessons. Choose fabric in a colour to co-ordinate with the skirt and top and one which will also allow you to wear the jacket over the dress. This doesn't necessarily mean an uninspiring beige, or a safe navy. Experiment with colour! Take scraps of material from your other clothes with you when you go to choose the jacket fabric and you will be surprised at the effect colours have on each other. Some colours have the effect of bringing others to life and making them appear glowing and vibrant, as when an artist highlights a painting in white. Others appear insipid, losing any depth or impact. So choose a colour to 'tie in' your wardrobe in a positive and vital way. Forget about never wearing certain colours together and be adventurous in your choice.

Choose a heavier fabric than you have worked with before. You will find, surprisingly, that wool, wool velour and wool mixtures are all easier to stitch and to handle than cotton and they also press well. Linen, gaberdine and denim are not quite so easy but would still be a good choice. Any fabric with a textured surface makes life easier than a plain, smooth surface. This is because any irregularities in the stitching are hidden in the weave and textured surfaces do not glaze in pressing as, for example, plain black and navy gaberdine may do.

Buy the best fabric you can afford. This is a trite statement, but it is sound advice. You are now reasonably proficient in making your own clothes and no doubt discovering the range of delightful fabrics available in the shops. Some are very expensive and, to my mind, well worth paying for. Really good fabric does half the work for you! It not only looks better, but it wears and keeps its shape much longer and is a delight to work with. You have now reached the stage where you no longer need be afraid of cutting into expensive fabric, so revel in choosing fabric you will really appreciate as you make it up and every time you wear it.

There is a wide choice of jacket styles in the STYLE catalogue, from classic, tailored designs to sporty blazer styles and casual blouson jackets to team with trousers or a skirt. You can choose any of these designs, any collar style and any type of sleeve, because, in this lesson you will learn to tailor a collar and revers, set in a sleeve with a smooth head and shoulder pads, make lined pockets, and learn more about making your clothes fit you.

Choose your jacket pattern by your bust size. Check the finished length, which is given on the back of the pattern envelope, with the skirt or dress you will wear with it. Refer to page 11 for shortening or lengthening the pattern.

CUTTING OUT

Before you cut out your jacket, re-read Lesson Three. Examine your fabric for one-way design or nap, remembering that, although it is not immediately obvious, both velour and brushed denim are nap fabrics and must be cut out following a 'with nap' layout (see page 14).

Take care with the *placing* of checks as well as with matching. Make sure that the finished hem of the jacket will complete a check and that the jacket fronts, when closed with the centre lines on top of each other, also complete the pattern. It is not possible to match the sleeve all round the armhole, but try to balance the line of the check at the front armhole notch. The collar should also be cut so that both ends are on the same check.

Thread mark the jacket accurately, following the advice given for the shirt blouse in Lesson Eleven.

As with the dress, the easiest way to start is to stitch the shoulder seams and then deal with the collar.

COLLAR AND REVERS

This type of collar, sometimes called a notched collar, requires exact stitching, firm and careful pressing and tailored top-stitching. It differs from the collars you have made before, in that the collar is not made up before it is attached. The revers are formed by turning back the facing, which is cut wider than usual.

With this type of collar particularly, make sure that you have transferred all the information you can from your paper pattern to your fabric.

You will see from the pattern piece that the jacket front seam allowance has to be slashed at the neckline. This is the point where the collar stops and the facing is attached to form the lapel. It is vital to cut this accurately.

First, reinforce the corner with a line of stay-stitching each side of the dot indicating the slash, about 1.2 cm (½ in) each side and on the seam allowance line. Clip the seam turning to the dot, almost to the stitching line (Fig 12.1). If the fabric frays oversew the raw edges.

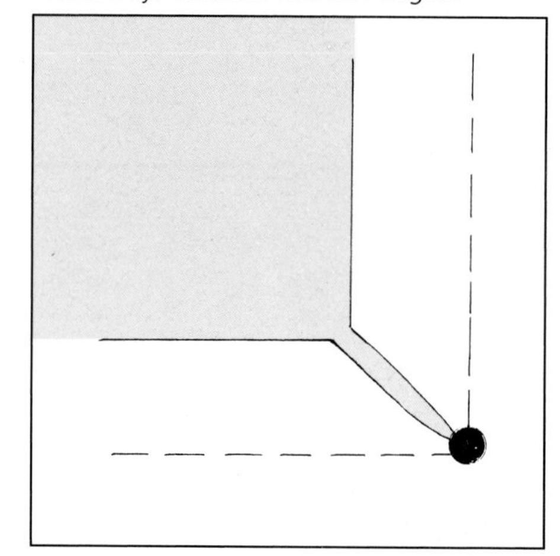

With the right sides together, pin one collar to the jacket, matching all the marks and notches. (Take care with this: it is very easy to put on a straight collar upside down!) Tack and stitch this collar to the neck edge between the given marks. Press the seam open. Do *not* trim the seam allowance (Fig 12.2).

Interface the other collar piece and the two front facings, following the instructions on page 48. Reinforce and clip the front facing, as before, where indicated, and reinforce with oversewing stitches if necessary. Neaten the long unnotched edge of the facing with a neat zig-zag stitch through fabric and interfacing, or with a narrow hem (Fig 12.3).

With the right sides together, pin the interfaced collar section to the two facing pieces, again taking care that the marks and notches correspond. Tack and stitch, taking the exact seam allowance (Fig 12.4).

Clip the collar at the point where the facing ends and turn under the seam allowance on the neck edge of the collar. Press this turning and press the seams open (Fig 12.5).

With the right sides together, pin the facings and collar section to the jacket, matching the cut edges and all the markings. Pin and tack.

Fig 12.1 Reinforce the corner before clipping to the dot.

Fig 12.2 Stitch one collar to the jacket edge. Do not trim the seam allowance.

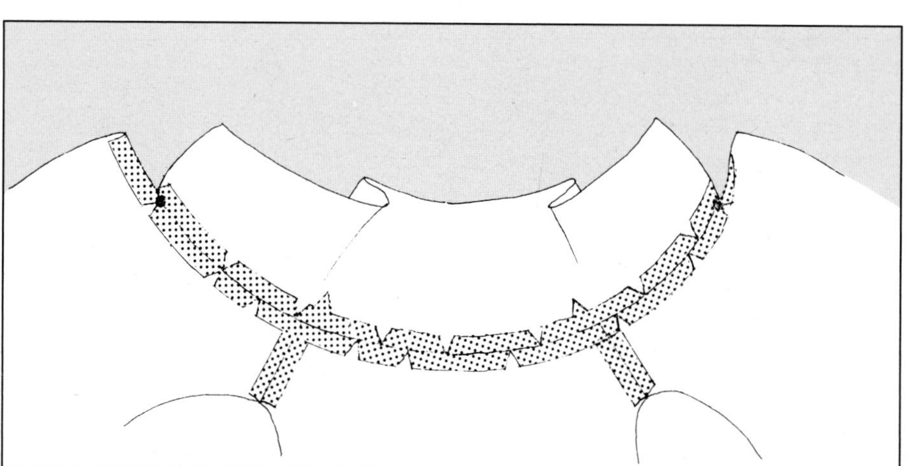

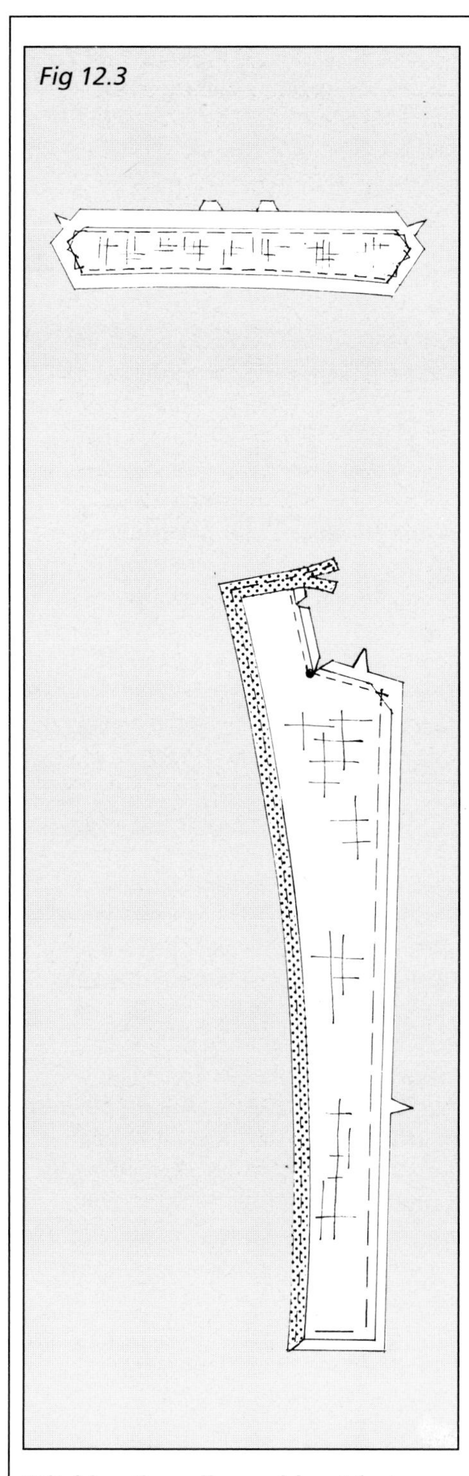

Fig 12.3 Interface one collar piece and the two front facings. Neaten the facing edge through the fabric and interfacing.

Fig 12.4 Stitch the collar to the facings, taking the exact seam allowance.

Fig 12.5 Clip the collar at the point where the facing ends.

Fig 12.6 Begin both lines of stitching from exactly the same spot.

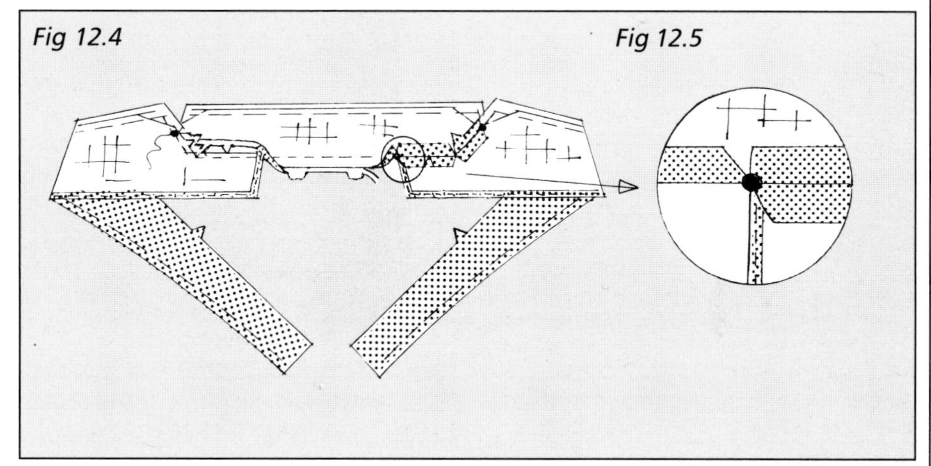

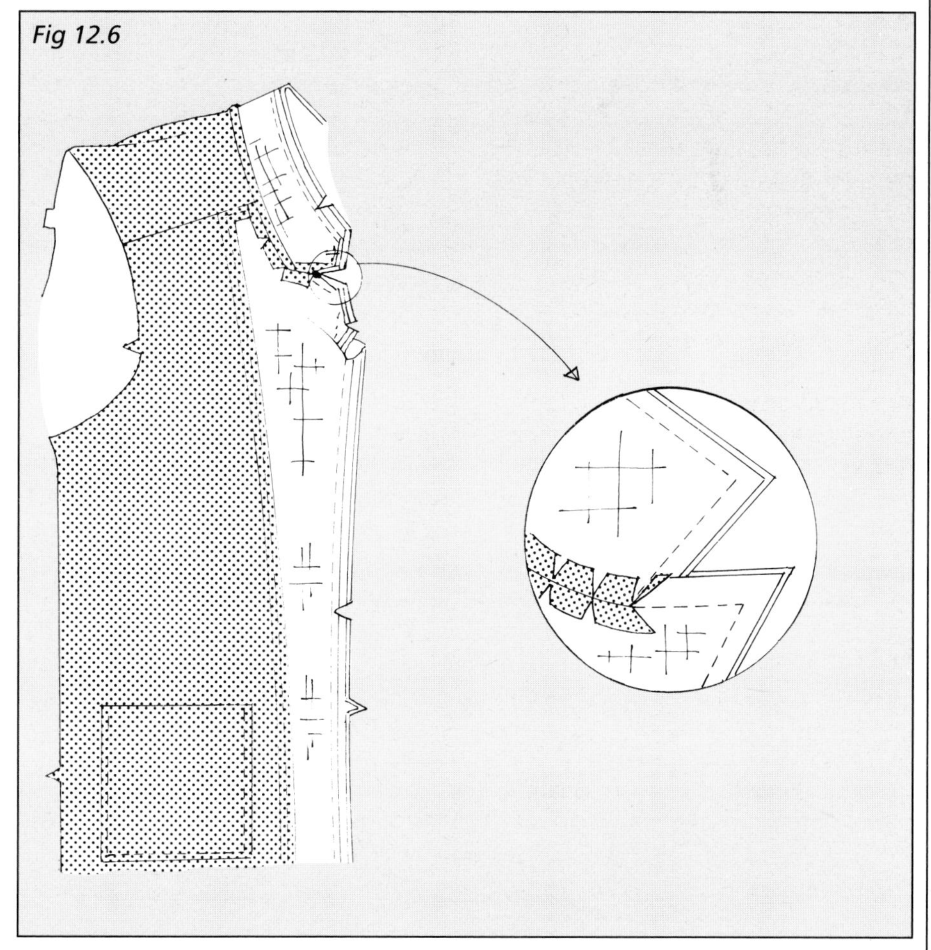

Stitching the collar and front facings

Stitching the collar and facings is best done as two separate operations. Stitch the collar first: starting from the slash, fold the seam allowance out of the way and stitch right round the collar edge. Then fold up the seam allowance on the facings and stitch the facings up and down the front edges. It is important to begin stitching from exactly the same spot for both operations (Fig 12.6).

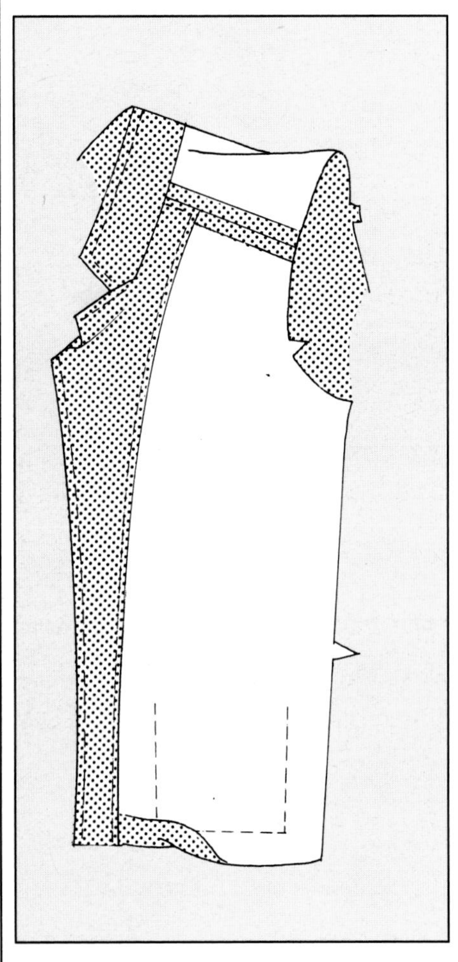

Fig 12.7 Edge-tack the collar and facings firmly in place.

Trim and layer the seams (see page 71). Cut off the corners of the collar. Turn the collar and facings to the inside. Work the seam between the finger and thumb so that it lies exactly on the edge, and edge-tack firmly in place (Fig 12.7).

Tack and hem the open edge of the collar at the centre back, down on to the neckline seam, enclosing the turnings.

Press the collar and facing three times in the same way as you pressed the shirt: that is, once on the right side with the tacking in, once on the wrong side, and then once again after you have removed the edge-tacking to press out any imprint of the thread.

Slip-stitch the top of the facing loosely to the shoulder seam.

Top-stitching can make all the difference to any jacket, and the collar, fronts, pockets and any emphasised seam lines, such as a raglan sleeve, should be top-stitched. On thick fabric, the top-stitching shows best if the line is 1.2 cm (½ in) away from the edge, rather than the more usual 6 mm (¼ in). Experiment with the various ways of top-stitching given on page 70. The top-stitching of the fronts of the jacket is done *after* the jacket hem has been turned up.

Some variations you will come across

Sometimes, a collar on an unlined jacket is put on with the addition of a curved, separate back neck facing. This is joined to the front facings at the shoulder seams. The procedure otherwise is the same, but the collar is not turned under and hemmed at the back neck as, of course, the facing neatens it.

On heavier fabric, the interfacing is applied to the *jacket* front and the *under*-collar, instead of to the facing and upper collar. Whether an interfacing is applied to the garment or to the facing, and whether the interfacing is on the outside of cuffs and collars or against the body, is often a matter of personal preference. You will find that if an interfacing is on the top piece of fabric, it conceals the seam turnings and gives a smoother finish; if it is applied to the underneath piece, there is no risk of an iron-on interfacing showing wrinkles after much wear and washing.

As a general guide, for medium- and heavy-weight fabrics for jackets and coats, apply the interfacing to the wrong side of the *jacket* and the *under*-collar. This is easier and less bulky when it comes to turning the facing to the inside after stitching. In most other cases, and with lightweight fabrics, apply the interfacing to the top collar and facings.

Fig 12.8 Cut off the top of the lining pocket on the fold line.

Fig 12.9 Stitch the pocket and lining, leaving a break in the centre of the stitching.

Fig 12.10 Stitch the three open sides of the pocket.

Fig 12.11 Slip-stitch the opening together.

LINED POCKETS

Deal with the pockets next, before you stitch the side seams; it is easier to attach them with the fabric flat on the table. If you have made any pattern alteration, this will affect the positions of the pockets and buttonholes. In this case, tack up the side seams and pin the pockets in place to check their position and adjust them if necessary. Remove the tacking.

Lining a pocket is the most satisfactory way of finishing a patch pocket on a jacket, whether it has a pocket flap or not.

Making the pockets
Cut two identical pocket shapes in fabric and in lining. Mark the fold line and stitching line.

Cut off the top of the lining pocket on the fold line (Fig 12.8).

Stitch the upper edges of the pocket and lining right sides together, taking the correct seam allowance and leaving a break in the centre of the stitching (Fig 12.9).

Fold the fabric pocket along the fold line. Pin the lining and pocket, right sides together, round the outside edges. Stitch the three open sides of the pocket (Fig 12.10). Trim the seam allowance to 6 mm (¼ in) and turn the pocket right side out through the opening. Ease out the corners gently using a pin, and edge-tack. Slip-stitch the opening together (Fig 12.11). Press the pocket.

Fig 12.8

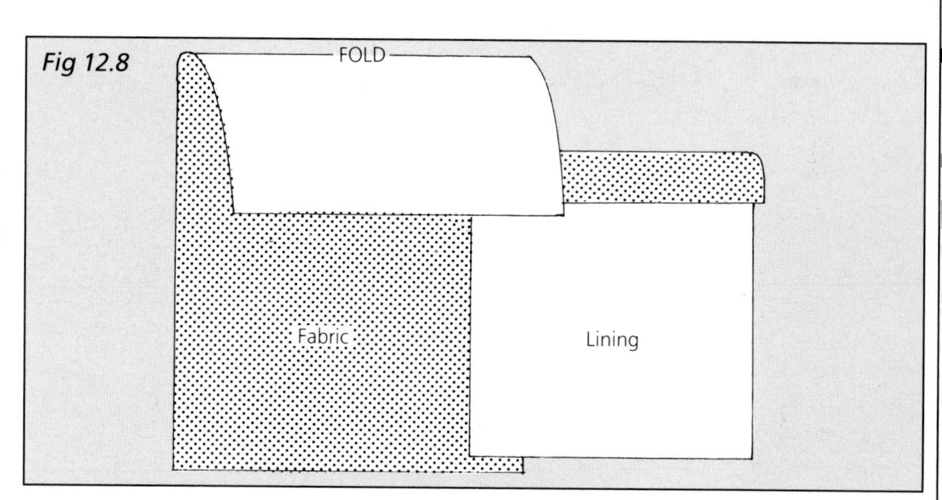

Fig 12.9

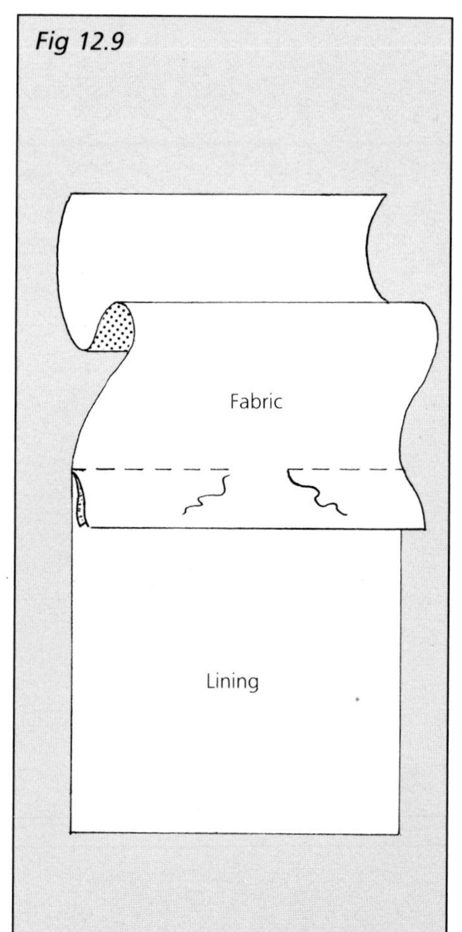

Fig 12.10

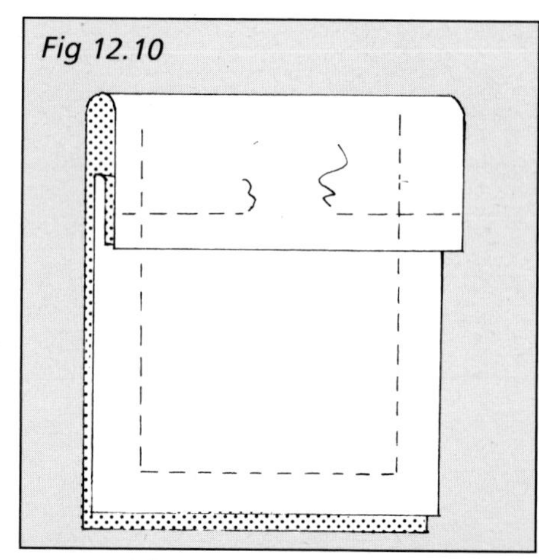

Fig 12.11

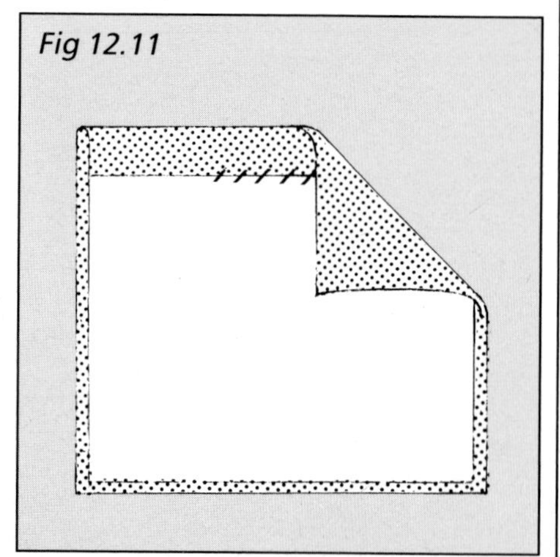

Attaching the pockets

The easiest way to achieve a neat finish to a pocket, especially with a bulky fabric, is to complete the pocket, top-stitch it and then sew it to the jacket, invisibly, by hand. Tack the pocket in place and stitch it, just under the outer edge (Fig 12.12). On lighter fabric, the pocket can be attached by the top-stitching (Fig 12.13).

Pocket flaps and welts

Flaps and welts on pockets are interfaced with lightweight interfacing and stitched, trimmed and turned in the same way as a collar. They should be top-stitched before they are stitched to the jacket front.

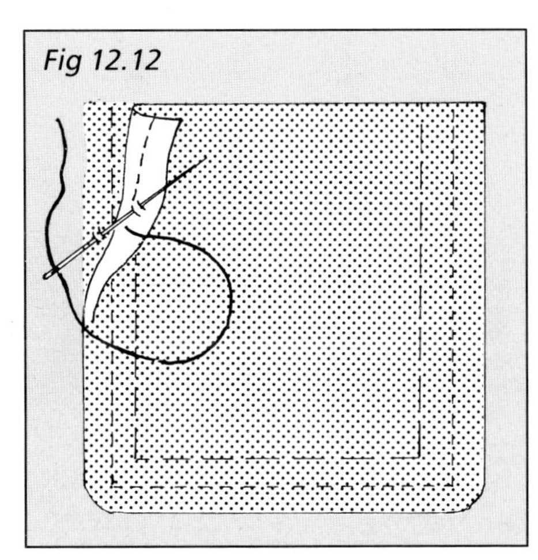

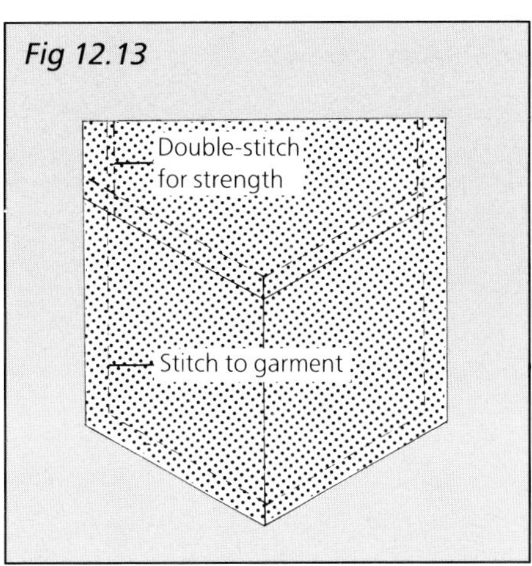

Fig 12.12 Hand-stitch the pocket just under the outer edge.

Fig 12.13 Lighter fabric pockets can be attached with the top-stitching.

FITTING THE JACKET

At this stage, try on the jacket over the top or dress you will wear with it. If the pattern has shoulder pads, slip them under the shoulder seams. Close the jacket with the centre front lines on top of each other and pin in place.

As with the dress, stand in front of a full-length mirror and check first that the collar is lying well and then turn back the facing the required amount to form the lapels. Hold these back with a pin. When the jacket is removed, the fold line for the revers will be pressed in *lightly*. (Do not press this fold line into a sharp crease, but leave it as a gentle roll over.)

Next, check the fit of the jacket over the bust, the waist and the hip. If it is a semi-fitted style and you are not happy with it, adjust the seam allowances and obtain the fit you would like by a process of trial and error. If you need a lot of alteration, you will find it easier to put on the jacket inside-out to pin the side seams, bearing in mind that the two halves of your body are not identical.

If you are still uncertain about the fit of your jacket, when you have adjusted and tacked the side seams, press them open and then try it on for a final fitting. This can sometimes make quite a difference.

Blouson and loosely fitting styles need very little, if any, fitting. They also have wide armholes and often dropped shoulder lines, which present no problem, but if yours is a set-in sleeve, you will have to check the fit of the armhole. Tack in both sleeves, using a small tacking stitch. (See 'Fitting the armhole', page 91).

INSERTING A SLEEVE

A smooth sleeve head needs care. As with all dressmaking procedures, if you take time to thread mark accurately and to match all the notches exactly, it presents no problem. But with setting in a smooth sleeve in particular, you will find that if you take less than the armhole seam turnings allowed, your sleeve will not fit.

It is a good idea to run a single line of coloured thread round the armhole on the seam line, joining up the tailor's tacking. Join the underarm sleeve seam and check that you have the following:

1 Two opposite sleeves, a right and a left.

2 Pronounced notches. There should be a single notch on the sleeve fronts and a double notch on the back, with corresponding notches on the armholes.

3 A thread mark on the sleeve head clearly marking the position for the shoulder seam. (This notch affects the hang of the sleeve and it was suggested you always mark this in red – see page 67.)

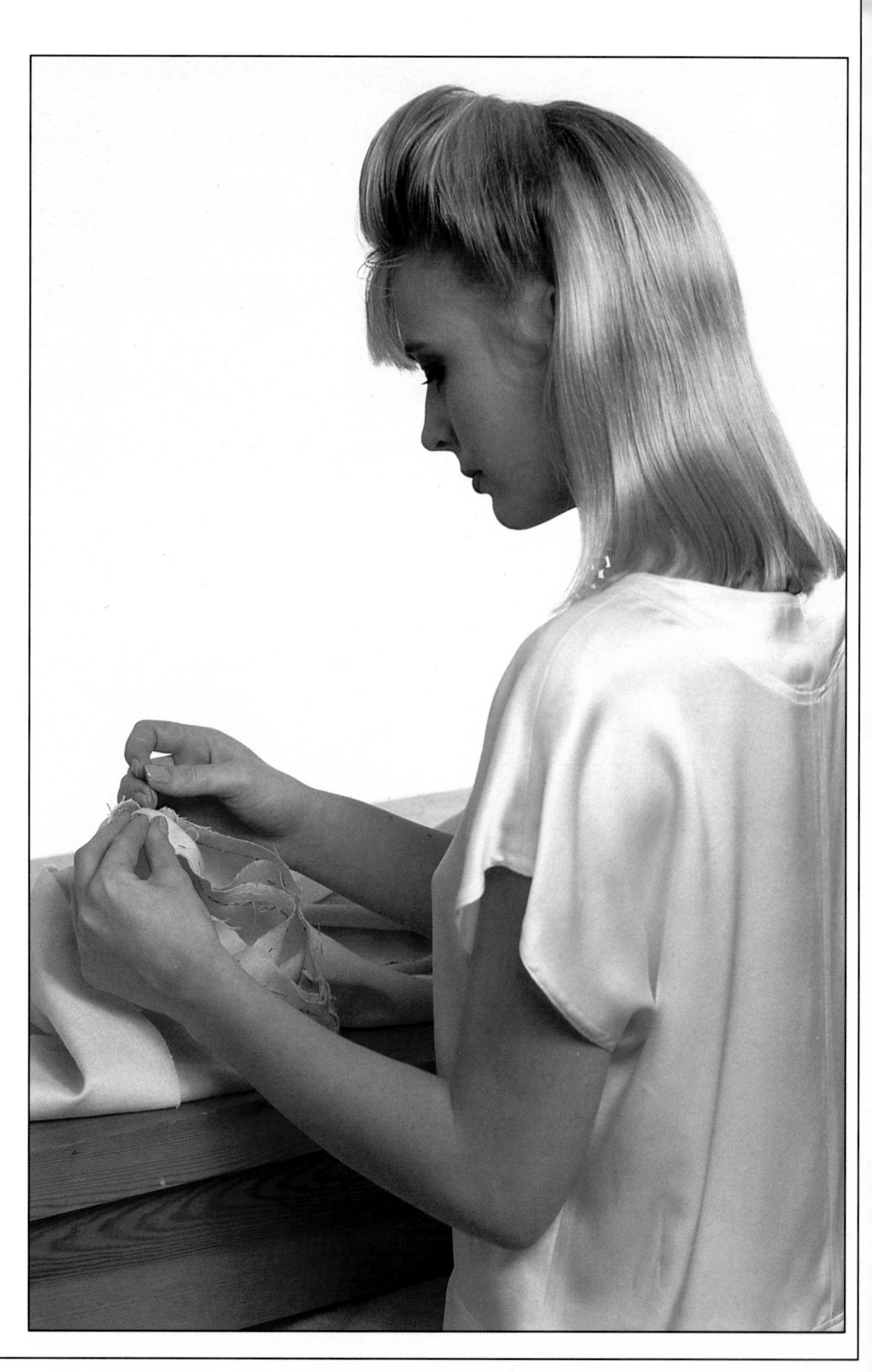

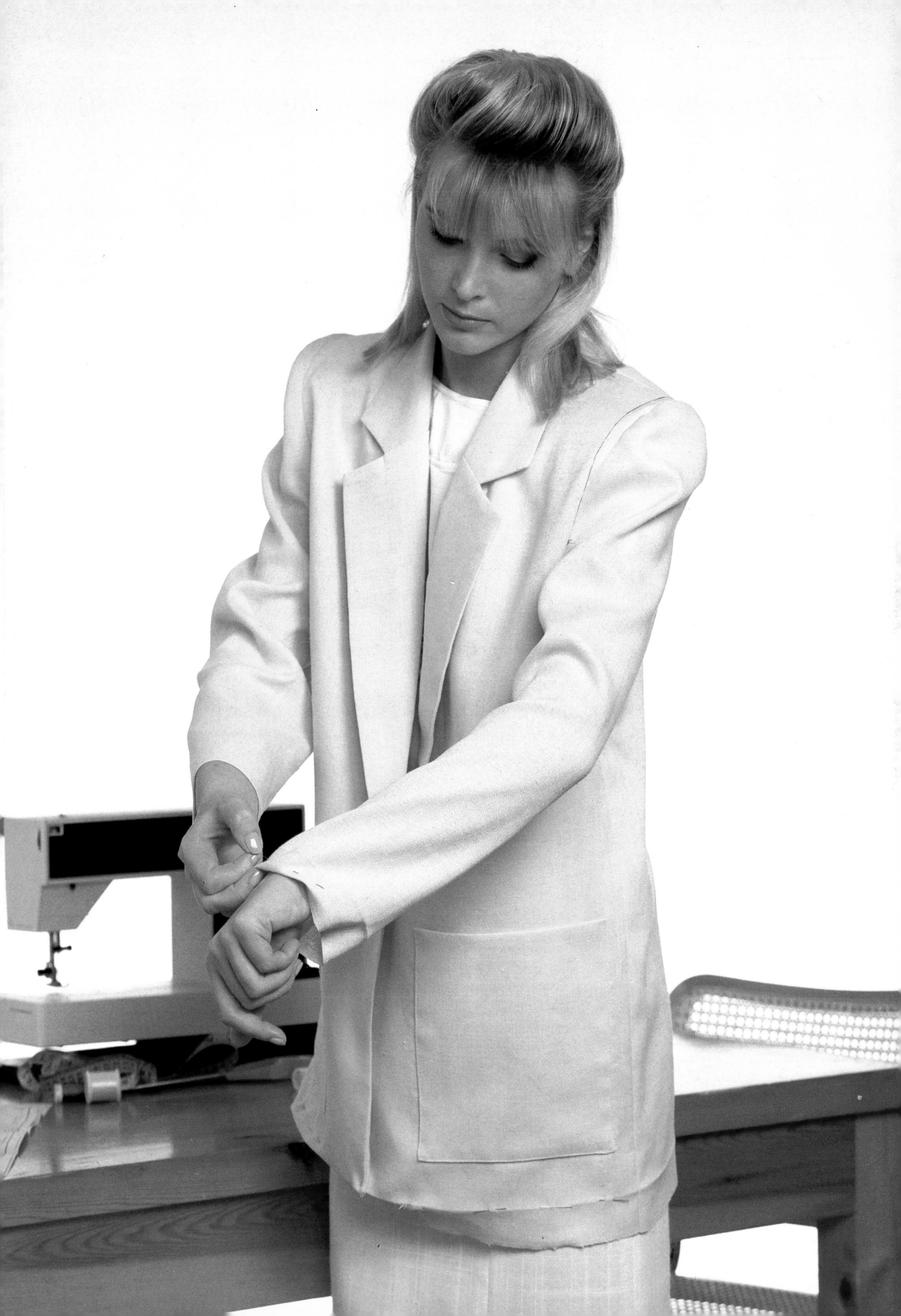

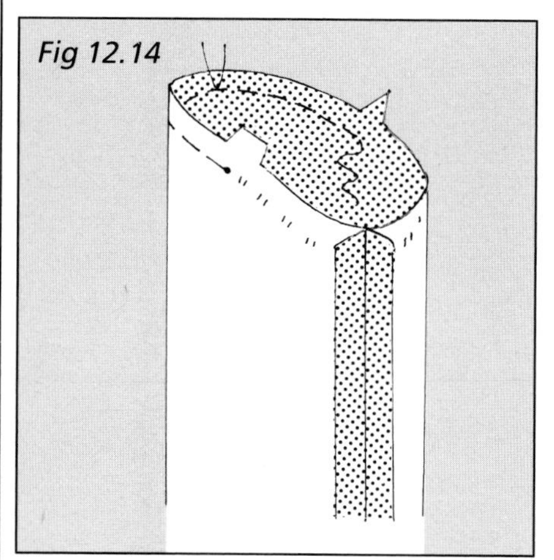

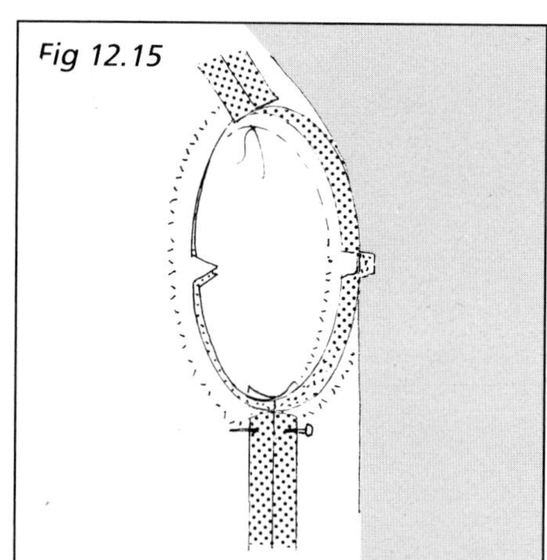

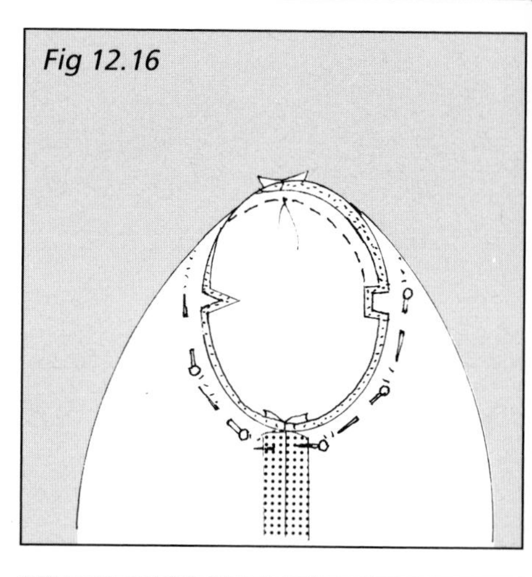

Use a single thread and work a row of tiny running stitches between the front and back notches on the sleeve head (Fig 12.14). For the gathered sleeve in Lesson Ten, two rows of stitching were used to gather up the surplus fabric. With a smooth sleeve head your are *not*, in fact, gathering; you are simply *easing* the yarns together to give a smoothly rounded top to the sleeve head. So, in practice, a single row of *tiny* stitches *on the stitching line* works best.

With the thread, draw up the fabric just a little over the sleeve head – only enough to shape the sleeve head slightly.

To make sure that you insert the sleeves correctly, put on the jacket, and put your arm into the appropriate sleeve. Hold the sleeve and jacket together at the underarm as you draw off the jacket (Fig 12.15).

With the jacket and sleeve still right side out, work from the inside (that is, looking into the armhole). Pin the underarm seams together as far as the notches on both sides (Fig 12.16).

Next, pin the thread mark at the top of the sleeve to the shoulder seam, placing the pin at right angles to the edge (Fig 12.17).

Now, working from this shoulder seam down to one notch, fold the sleeve head outwards into a curve, bending the fabric over your forefinger, raw edges away from you (Fig 12.18). Pin. This adjusts the sleeve fabric evenly and into gentle curves.

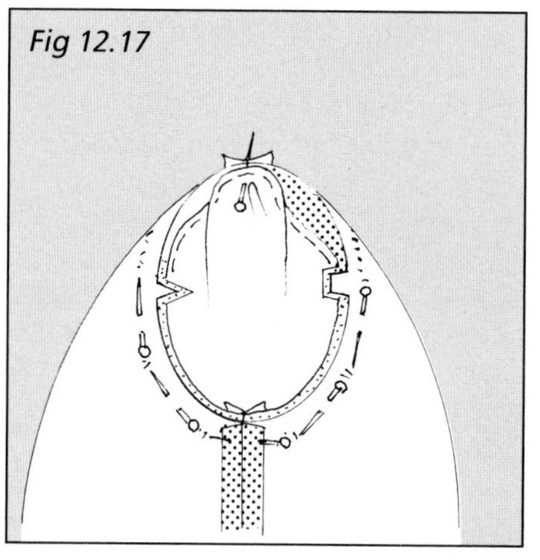

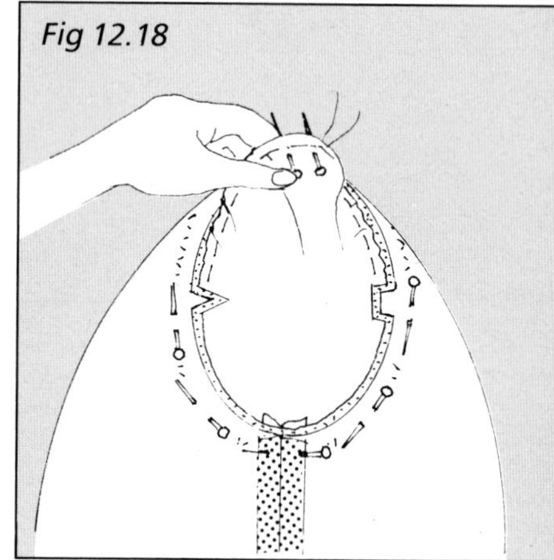

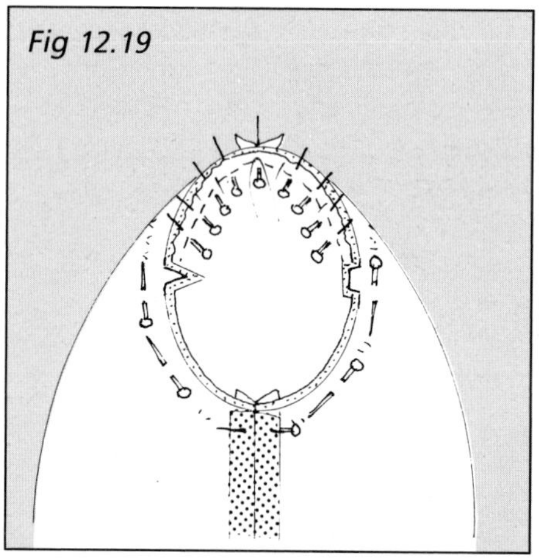

Fig 12.19

Go back to the first pin and work down the other side to the notch in the same way (Fig 12.19).

Tack round the armhole with a small stitch on the seam line. Try on the jacket to check the fit of the sleeve.

Fig 12.14 Work a row of tiny stitches over the sleeve head.

Fig 12.15 Hold the sleeve and jacket together at the underarm.

Fig 12.16 Pin the underarm seams as far as the notches.

Fig 12.17 Pin the top of the sleeve.

Fig 12.18 Bend the fabric over your forefinger.

Fig 12.19 Work down to the notch in the same way.

FITTING THE ARMHOLE

You may sometimes find that a pattern size will give you a good fit at the bust, waist and hip, but that your shoulders are narrower than average and that the pattern is too wide for you across the shoulders. This means that, when you insert the sleeve, the jacket hangs off the edge of your shoulders and the whole thing looks far too big.

Altering the sleeve line so that it is correct for you is not easy to judge, but it is something that you must master in order to get a neat, tailored fit at the shoulder. As with all fitting, it is learned by trial and error and becomes easy with practice.

Stand square-on to the mirror with your arms down by your sides and assess your shoulder width. Is the edge of the sleeve head dropping in line with your own upper arm or is it projecting beyond it and generally looking too big? The illustration on your pattern envelope is a good guide to the finished 'look' of the garment. In some garments, the shoulder width is deliberately emphasised and over-large.

But if yours is a classic style and has a normal shoulder line and you feel it is too wide for you, remove the tacking which holds the sleeve between the front and back notches over the sleeve head. Ease the sleeve head on to your shoulder a little further in. Hold it in place with a pin on the shoulder seam and adjust both shoulders this way. Stand back and take a look at the effect and experiment until you are happy with the result. Often only minimal adjustment is required: 6 mm (¼ in) or less can make all the difference (Fig 12.20).

Now, where the fold of the sleeve head touches the shoulder, use sharp tailor's chalk or a row of pins to define the new shoulder line. (You will probably need help to mark the line at the back.) Concentrate on getting one armhole edge exactly right and then remove the jacket, fold the two armholes inside one another and thread mark them to transfer the new line from one side to the other.

Then trim the seam allowance over the sleeve head to 1.5 cm (⅝ in) and stitch the sleeve, following the same procedure as for the gathered sleeve in Lesson Ten.

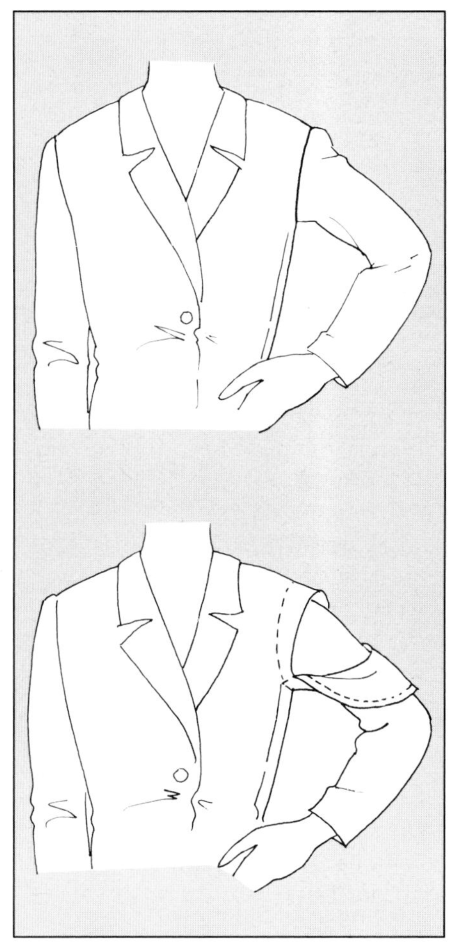

Fig 12.20 A minor adjustment at the armhole can make all the difference.

SHOULDER PADS

Shoulder pads are used to give a squared and tailored look to a classic jacket as well as being used as a fashion detail. They are set well into the edge of the sleeve to support the armhole seam (Fig 12.21) and centred beneath the shoulder seam.

Covering a shoulder pad

Covering a shoulder pad is trickier than it might appear as you must not flatten the thickness of the pad. To make a 'bag' and insert the pad into it does not work well. It adds extra bulk and the extra seams may show through as a ridge on the right side of the garment.

The neatest way to cover a shoulder pad is to place it flat on a remnant of fabric at least twice its size and fold the fabric over the thickness of the pad (Fig 12.22). Pin and tack it to the pad round the outside edges and trim away the surplus fabric. Then stitch the outside edges through all thicknesses with a neat zig-zag stitch (Fig 12.23).

Attaching a shoulder pad

Fold the pad in half and pin the half-way mark to the shoulder seam, with the thickness of the pad projecting into the sleeve head by the same amount as the armhole seam turnings. Stitch along the seam turnings through the thickness of the pad and the two layers of fabric using a stab stitch. Do not pull the thread tight as you must avoid flattening the pad.

Catch-stitch the opposite end of the pad to the seam turning with several long, loose stitches, so that the stitching does not form an indent on the right side of the jacket.

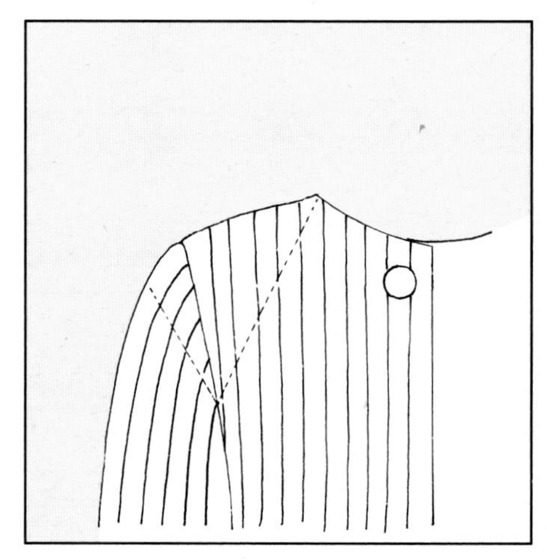

Fig 12.21 Shoulder pads are set well into the sleeve to support the armhole.

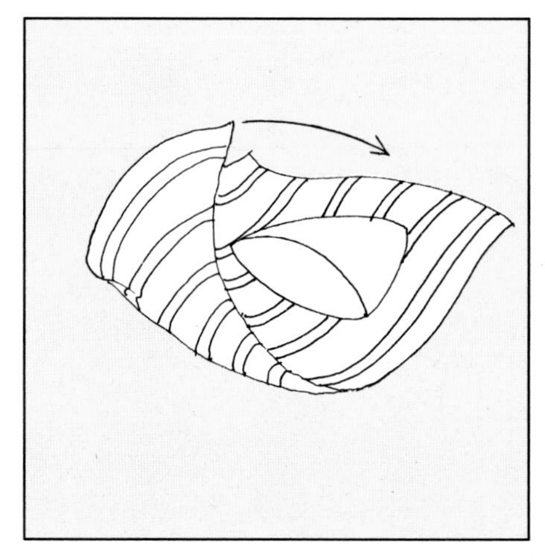

Fig 12.22 Fold the fabric over the thickness of the pad.

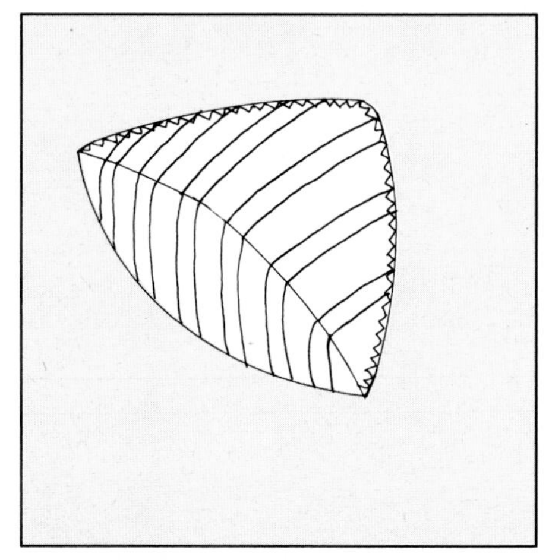

Fig 12.23 Stitch the outside edges with a neat zig-zag stitch.

THE JACKET HEM

Open out the front facing and measure and turn up the jacket hem. Tack it on the edge and press the fold lightly (Fig 12.24).

Trim away any surplus interfacing in the jacket hem to the fold line. Neaten the edge of the hem as for a skirt hem (see page 43) and catch-stitch in place. Turn back the facing and slip-catch the facing to the hem (Fig 12.25).

Top-stitch the jacket.

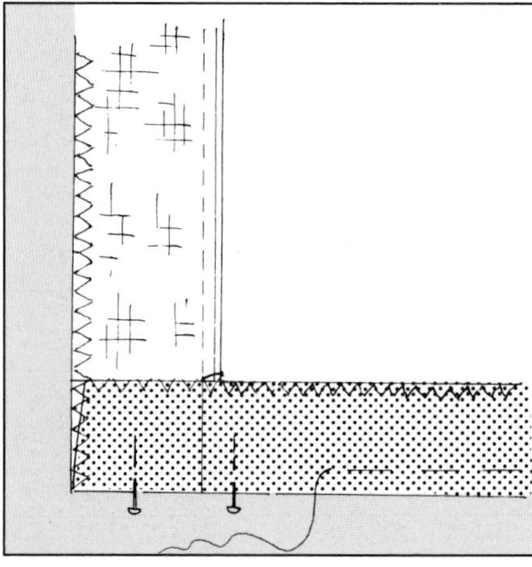

Fig 12.24 Tack the edge of the hem and press the fold lightly.

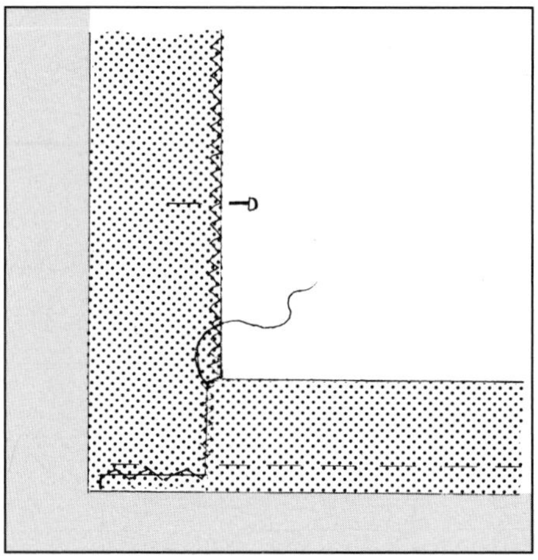

Fig 12.25 Slip-stitch the facing to the hem.

The perfect finish

So you have come to the end of this dressmaking course. I hope that you have followed the careful instructions for the different dressmaking procedures and that you are happily wearing your new outfit!

You may have noticed that no short cuts to dressmaking have been included in this book. This is because, in fact, there is none. There is no quick way to get a perfect finish on your clothes. There *are* quick ways to put sections of fabric together to get something to wear! But the aim of this book is to teach you to produce well-finished clothes that you can wear with confidence. The expert dressmaker *can* take short cuts.
And when you are a competent and experienced dressmaker, you will find your own short cuts without my help!

I also hope you have found these sewing lessons enjoyable and satisfying, but that you are not *entirely* satisfied. Because dressmaking is a continuing creative hobby, your skills improve with practice and you learn more with every item that you make. The more you learn, the more satisfying the results.

Start now to be critical of the finish of your clothes. Look out for such things as a carelessly finished hem, showing as a ridge or a row of dimples on the right side of a skirt; unevenly matched checks and badly positioned floral designs; collar ends of uneven length; sleeve heads which are puckered and not smoothly rounded. All these things advertise the fact not that you made it yourself, because the clothes you buy can be badly finished, but that whoever made it made it badly.

And take care with accessories for the clothes you make. Enjoy looking round for exactly the right belt to complete an outfit. Choose good buttons and experiment with colour, size and interesting shapes. Look at scarves to contrast or complement your outfit, and keep an eye on the wide selection of braids and trims that appear in the shops.

And since you can convince yourself that you are saving money by making your own clothes, you can afford to indulge yourself a little with your choice of just the right shoes to give a good line to the skirt and the latest designs in colour-matched tights and unusual handbags.

Any creative hobby in which the mind is concentrated and stilled is a boon. And dressmaking is just this. When it is combined with an understanding of good design and expert needlework, then working with fabric becomes an art.

Index